works of
daniel cordani

THE INFECTED NUCLEUS

texts of
robert booras

Established in 2000, **UpSet Press** is an independent, not-for-profit (501c3 tax-exempt) press based in Brooklyn. The original impetus of the press was to upset the status quo through art and literature. The Press has expanded its mission to promote new work by new authors; the first works, or complete works, of established authors–placing a special emphasis on restoring to print new editions of exceptional texts; and first time translations of works into English. Overall, UpSet Press endeavors to advance artists' innovative visions and works that engender new directions in art and literature.

UpSet Press

PO Box 200340
Brooklyn, NY 11220

www.upsetpress.org

Book design
Jessica D'Elena-Tweed

Library of Congress Control Number 2019947992
ISBN 978-1-937357-84-9
Printed in the United States of America

Sanity on the fringe of distorted
Who are they to just take shit and hoard it?
Who am I that I don't get my portion?

The most impressionable minds
get molested and informed by manipulating forces
Don't fret little man, don't cry

they can never take the energy inside you were born with
Knowing that, understand you could never be poor
You already won the war, you were born rich

You can only take the energy you had
Going back to the realm or the home where your lord is
Whoever whatever that lord is couldn't

Give a fuck if you ever made fortunes
Fuck anyone ever tryin' to run that punk shit
Send 'em to the flames where the orcs live

Them and the lost minds thinking they're
smarter than us
Don't understand love's importance

And we can weaponize that, bring 'em back to the truth
Where the ashes and dust got formed in

// El-P

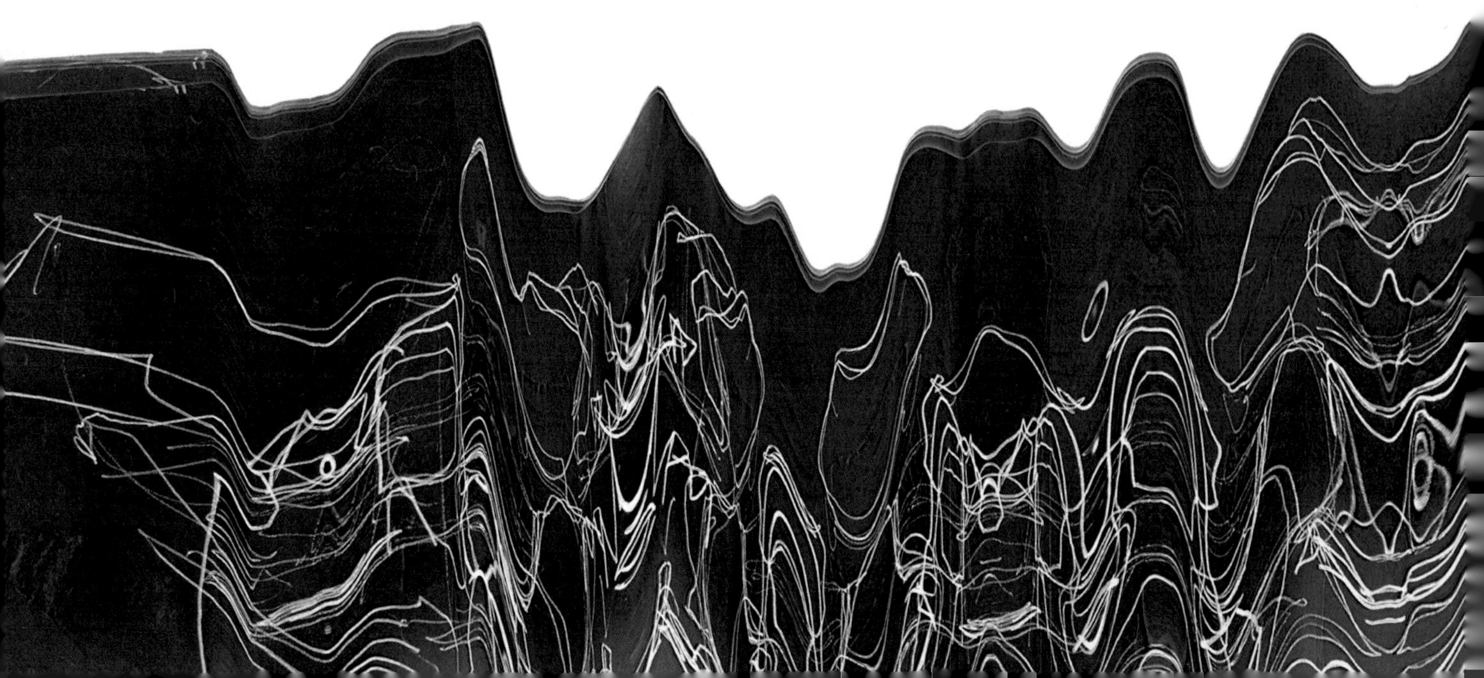

But when one has been tortured
to the point of becoming a nucleus,

then one starts demonicaly wanting
to serve the ritual, even if

the ritual means consuming oneself-
just as in order to have the incense

the only way to get it is to burn the incense.

// Clarice Lispector

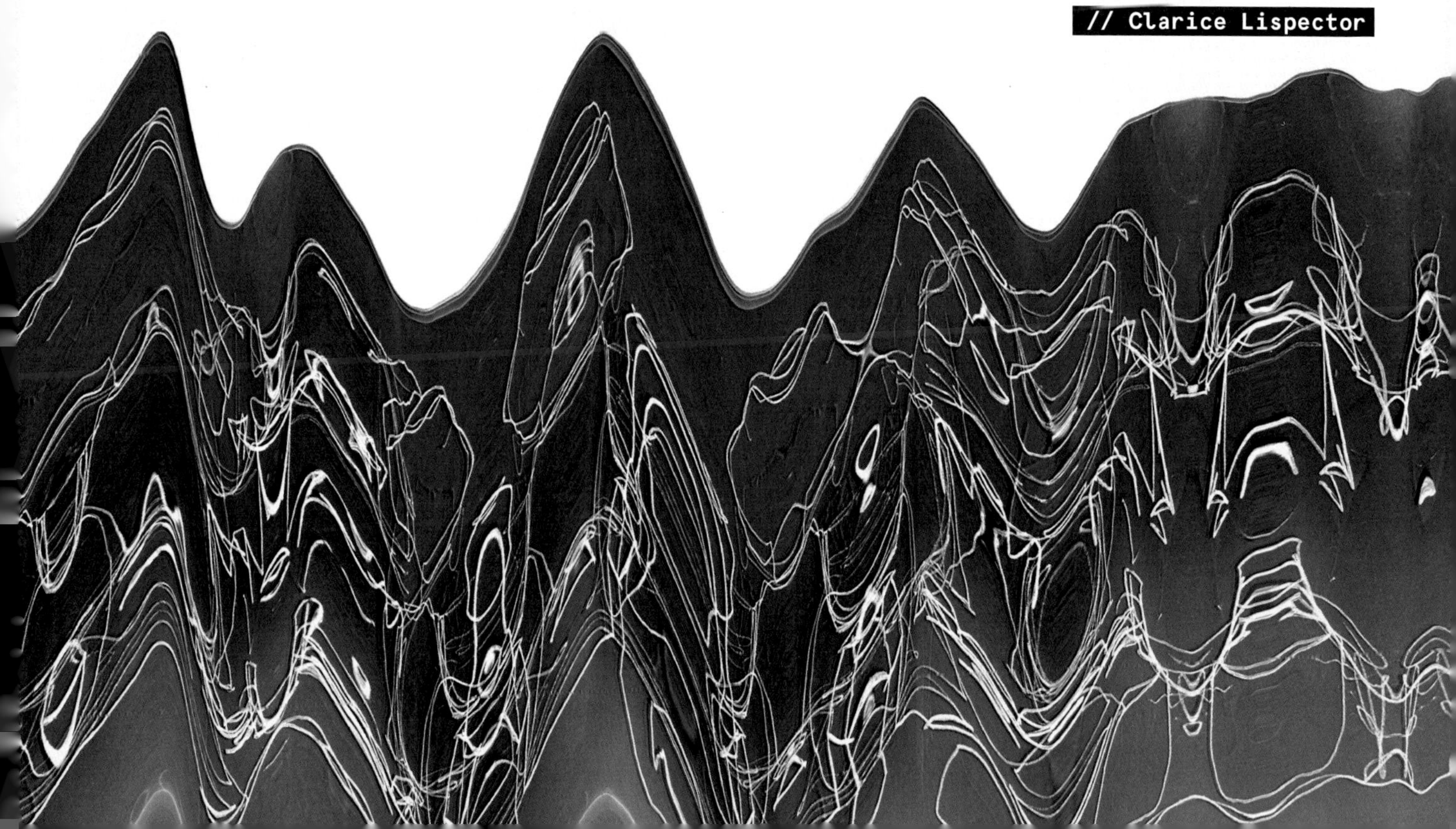

table of contents

OV

LOQUELA OF THE FATHER

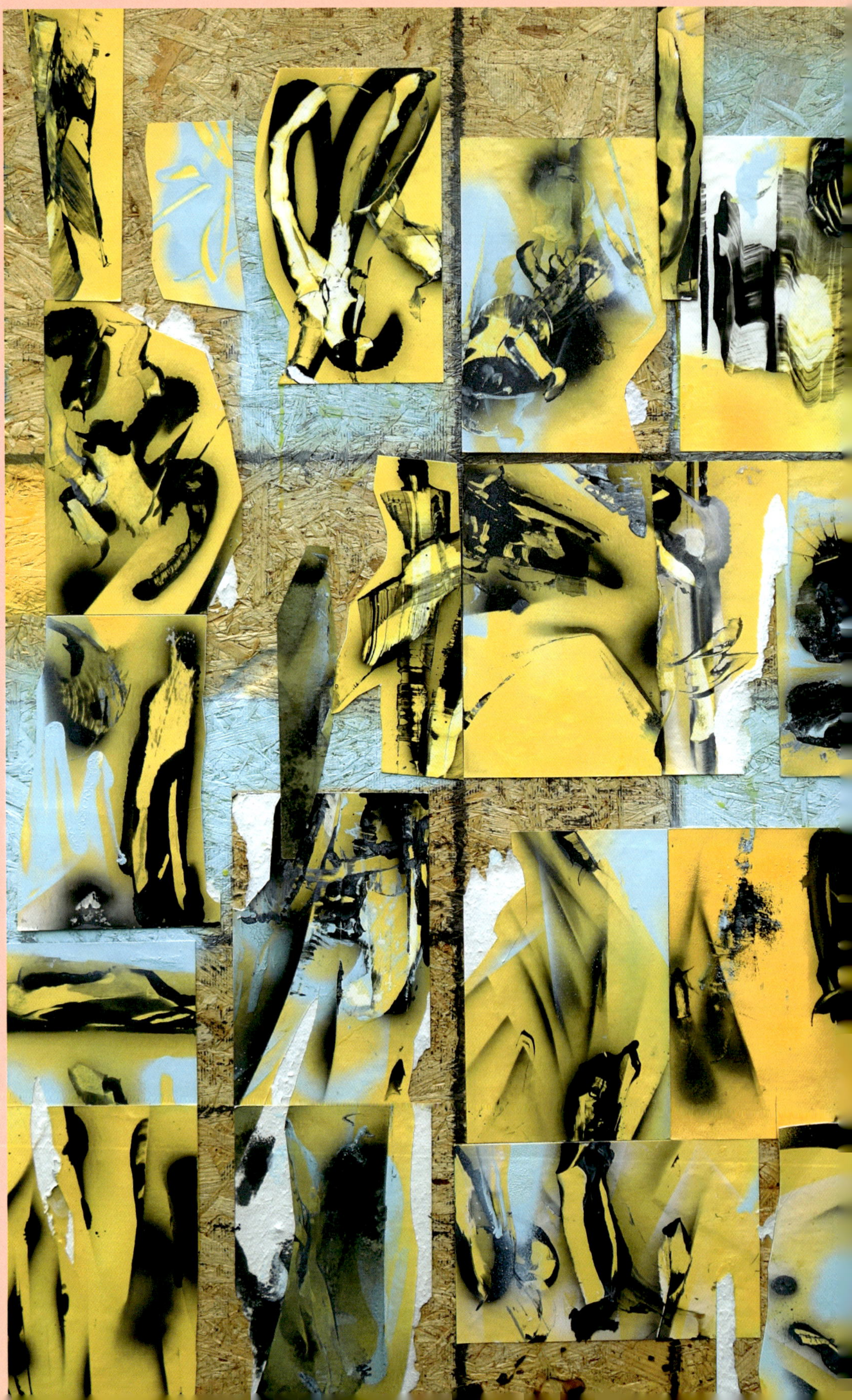

LOQUELA OF THE FATHER

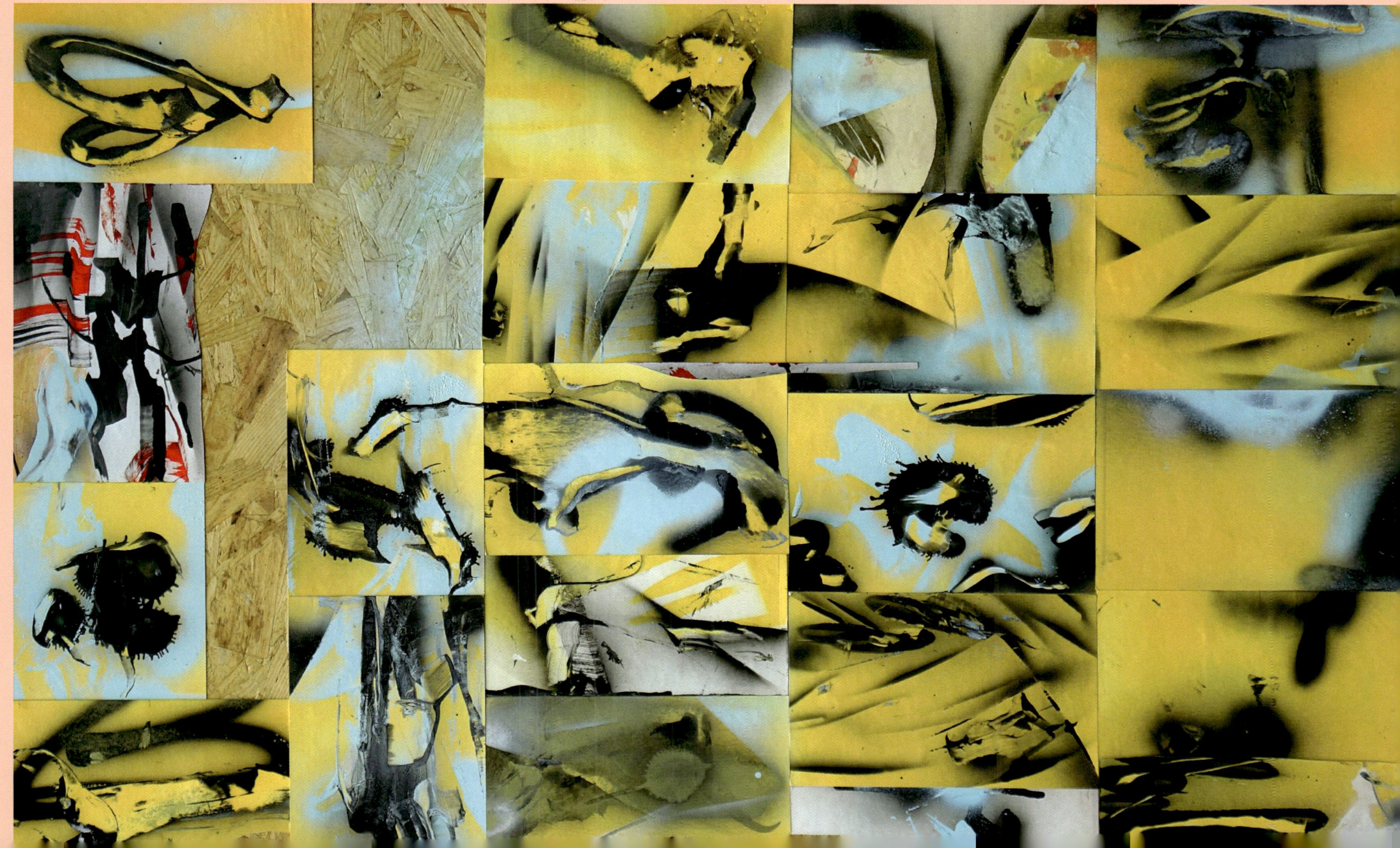

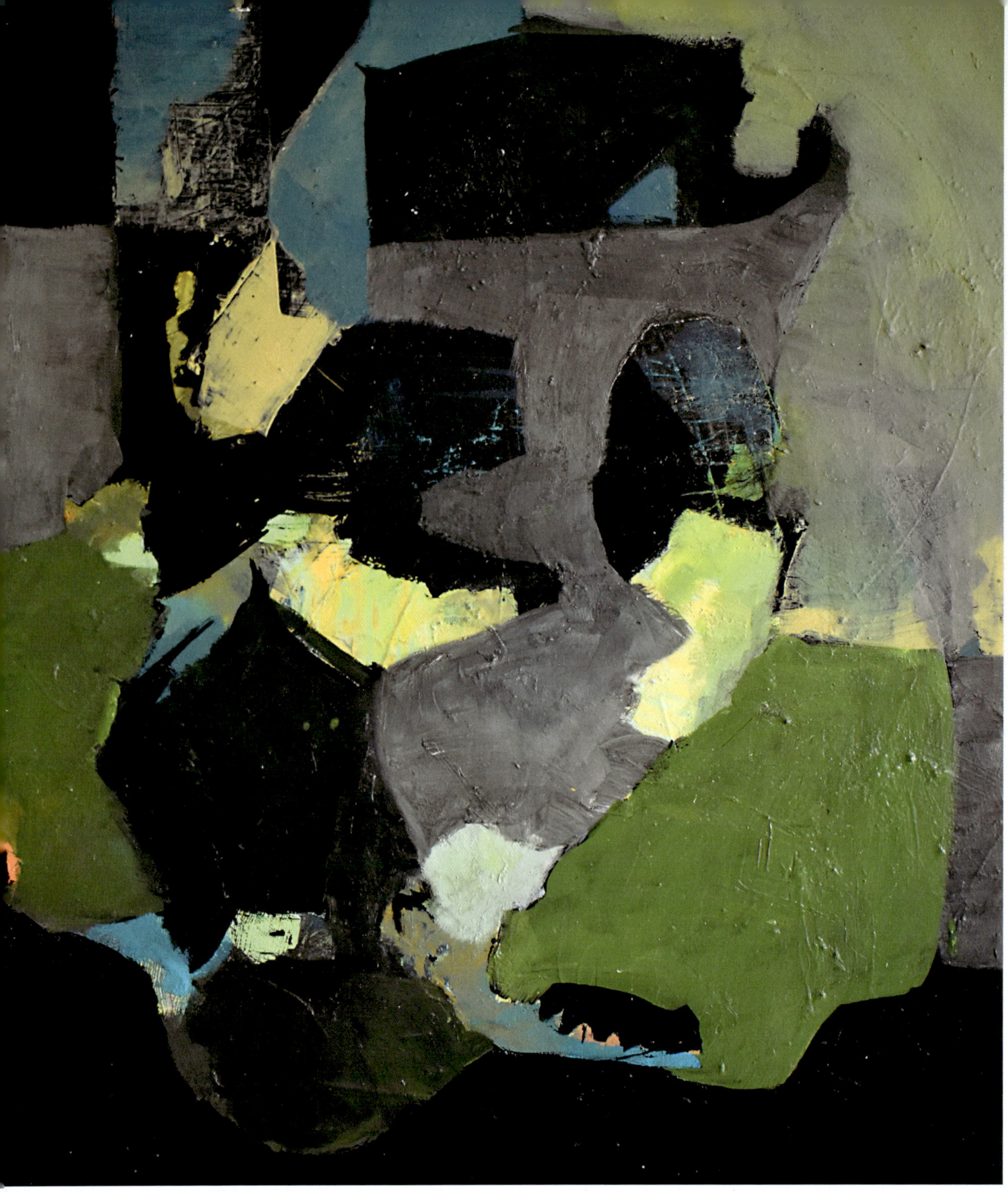

I organize a casting call.

I rent a loft in which to conduct the interviews.

I am one of the actors too.

I organize a casting call.

I rent a loft in which to conduct the interviews.

I am one of the actors too.

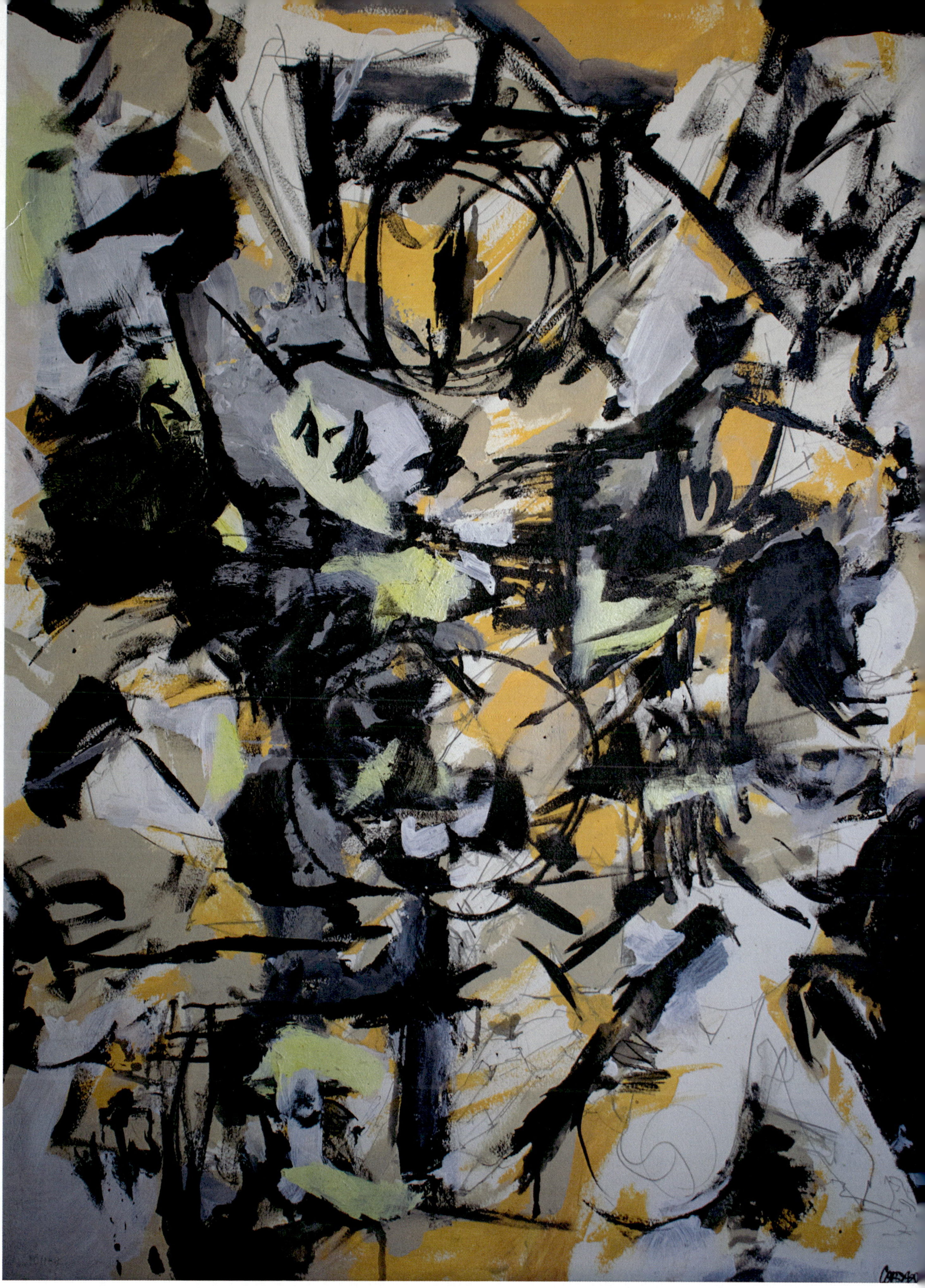

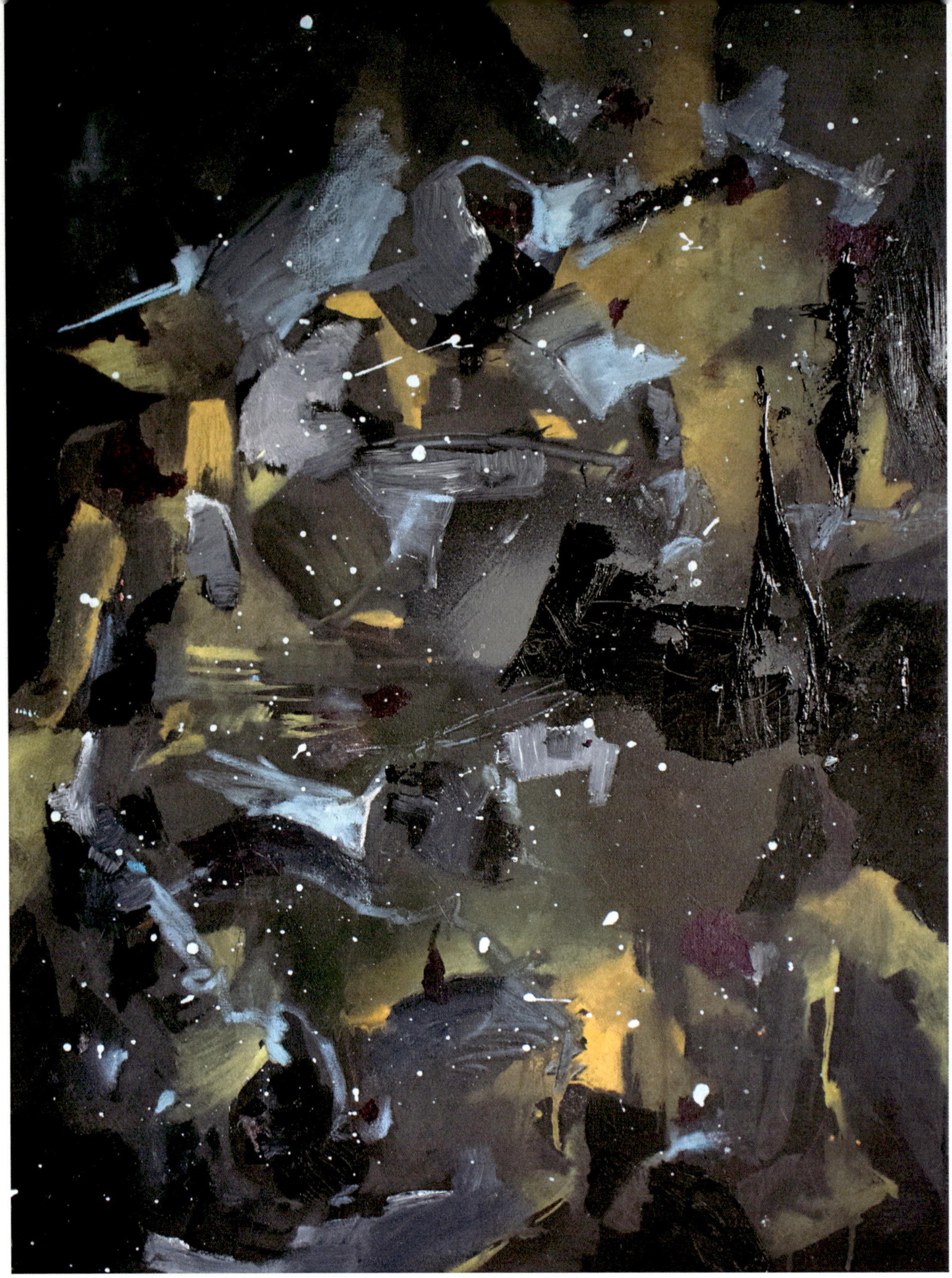

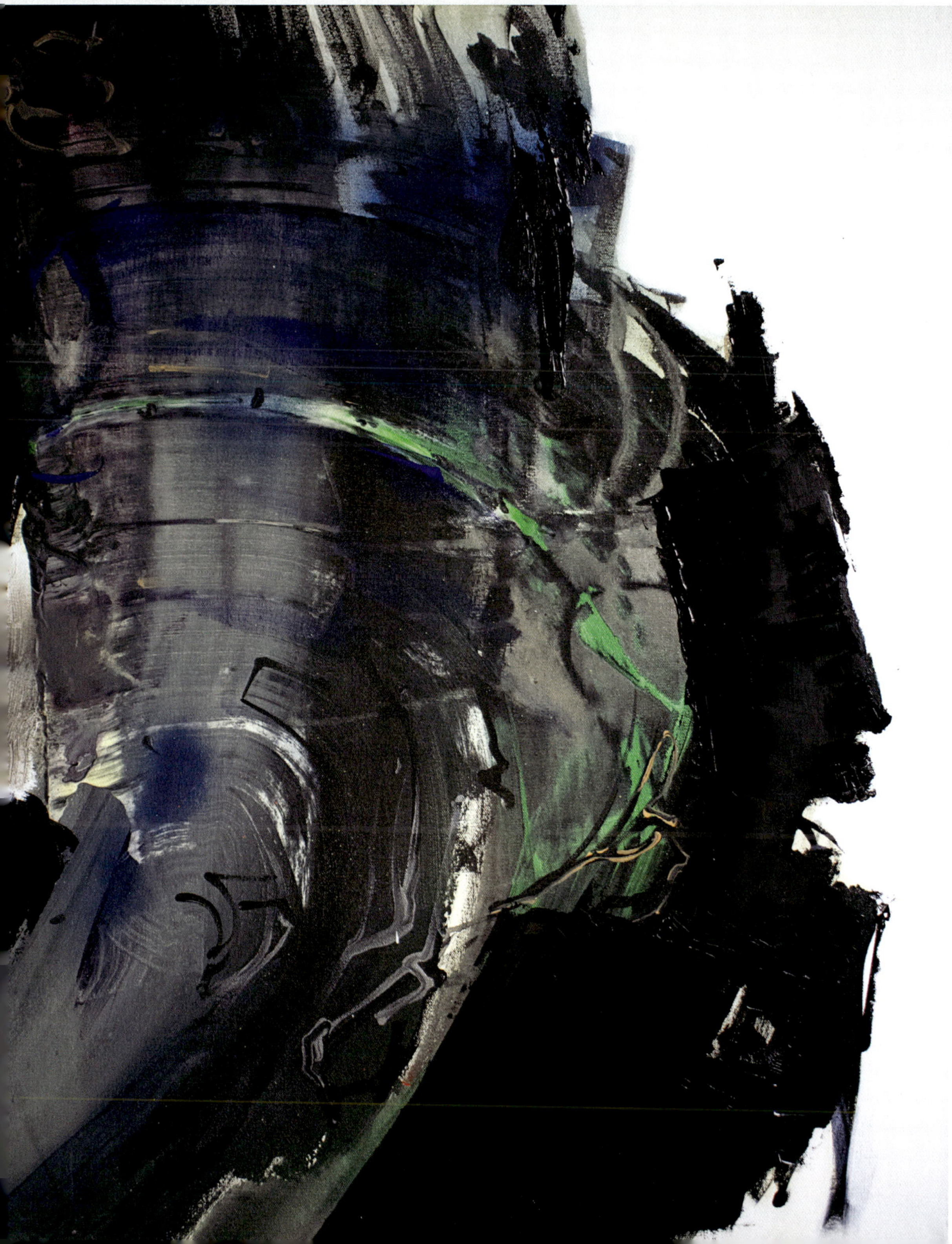

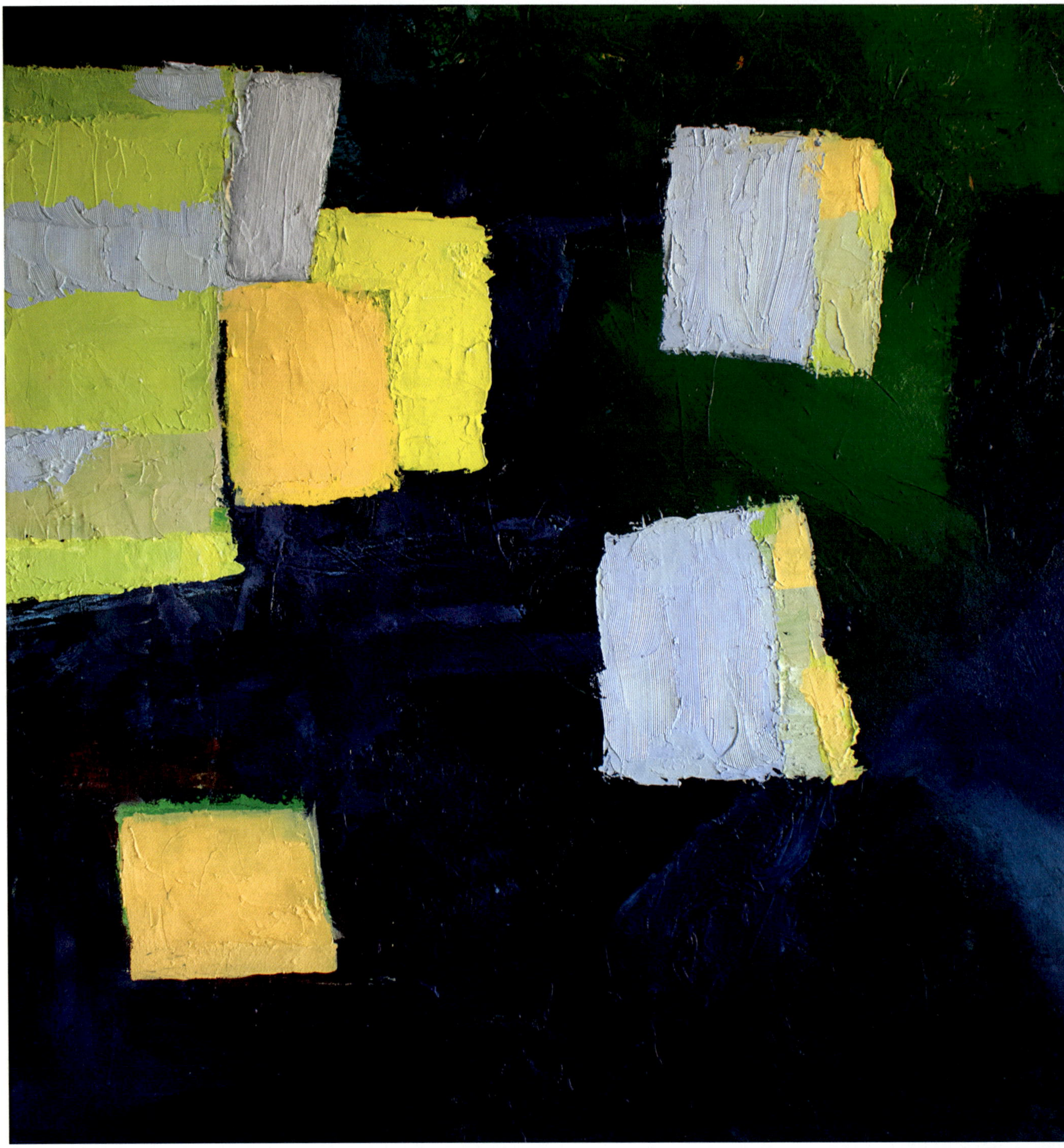

There is in fact only one role.

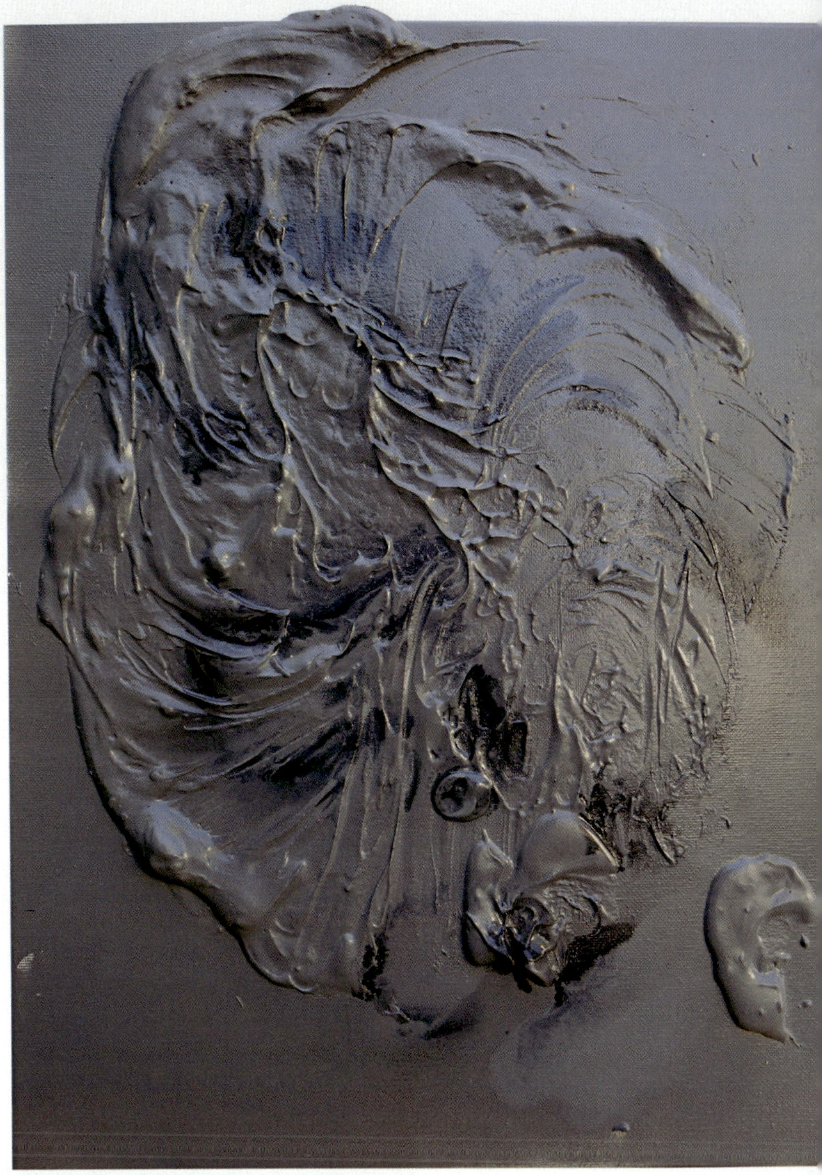

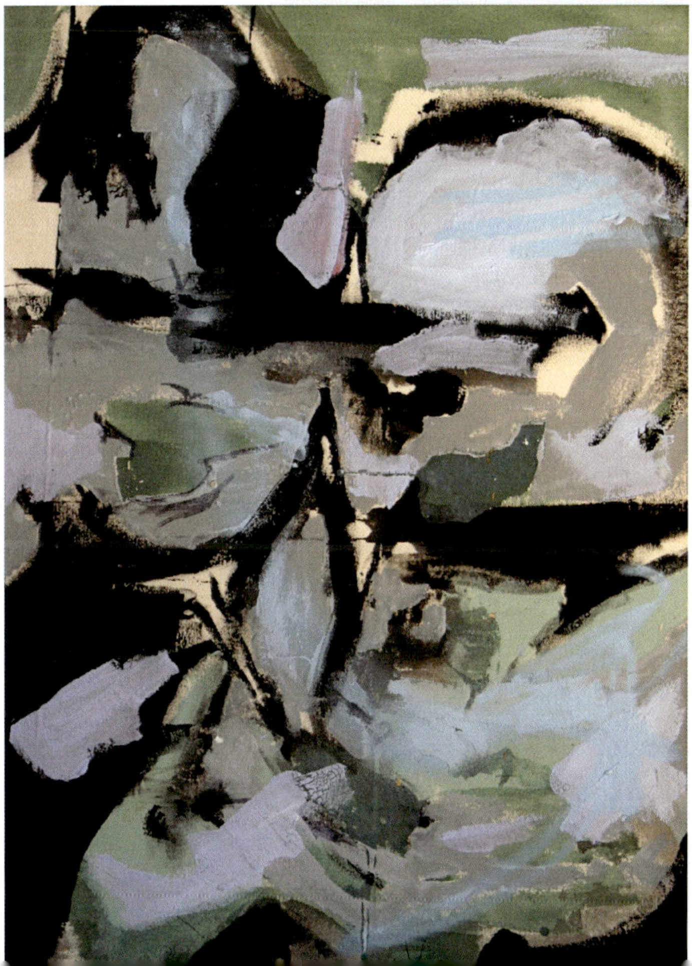

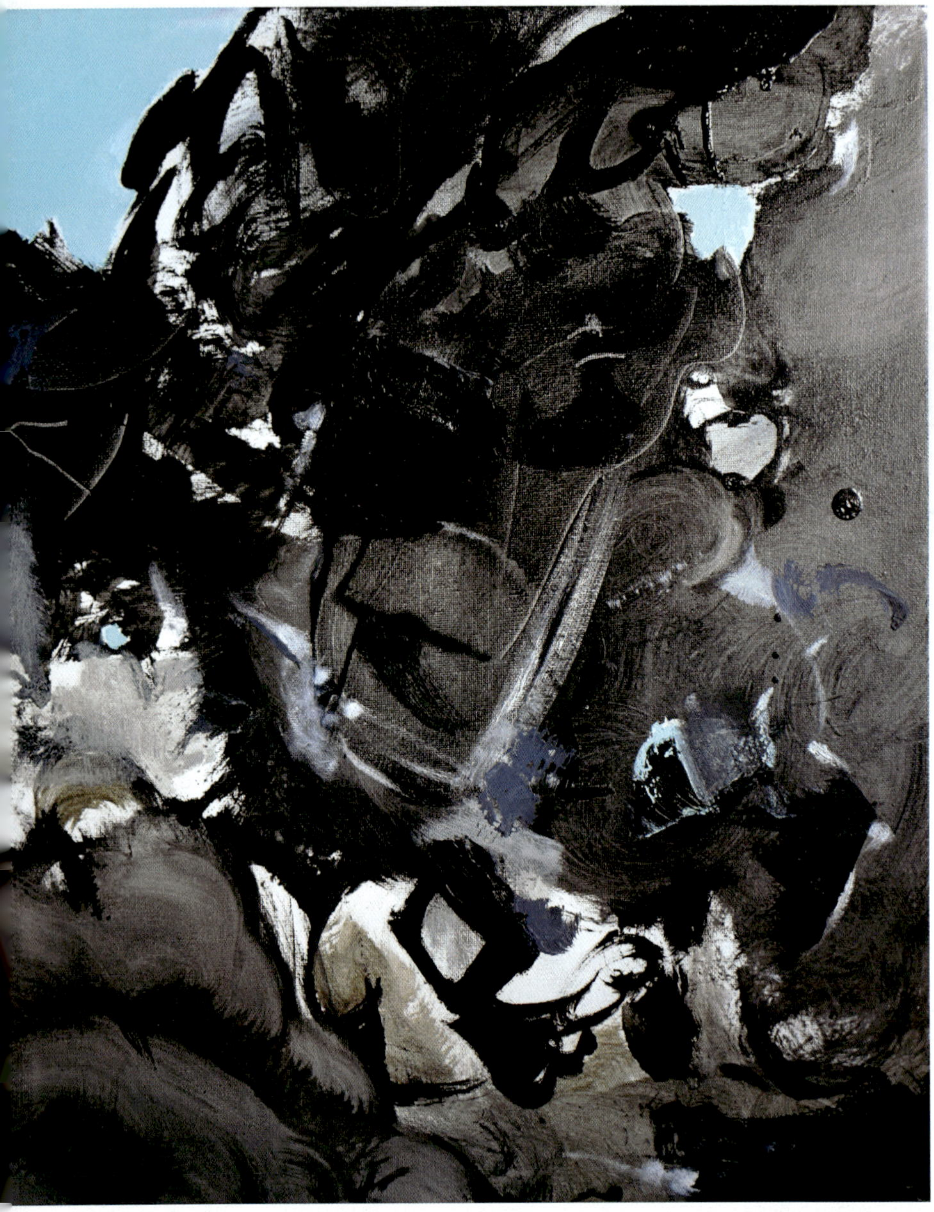

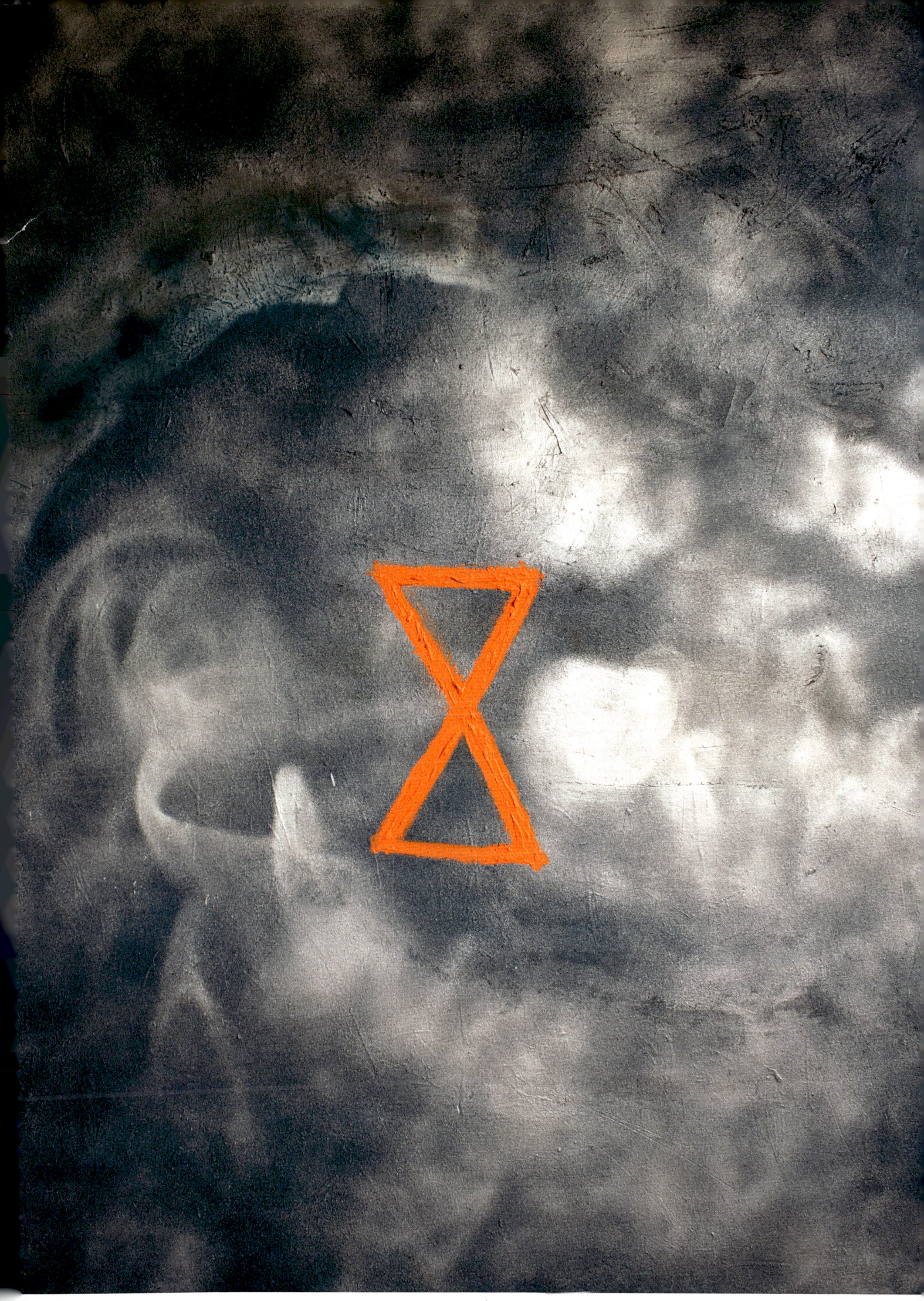

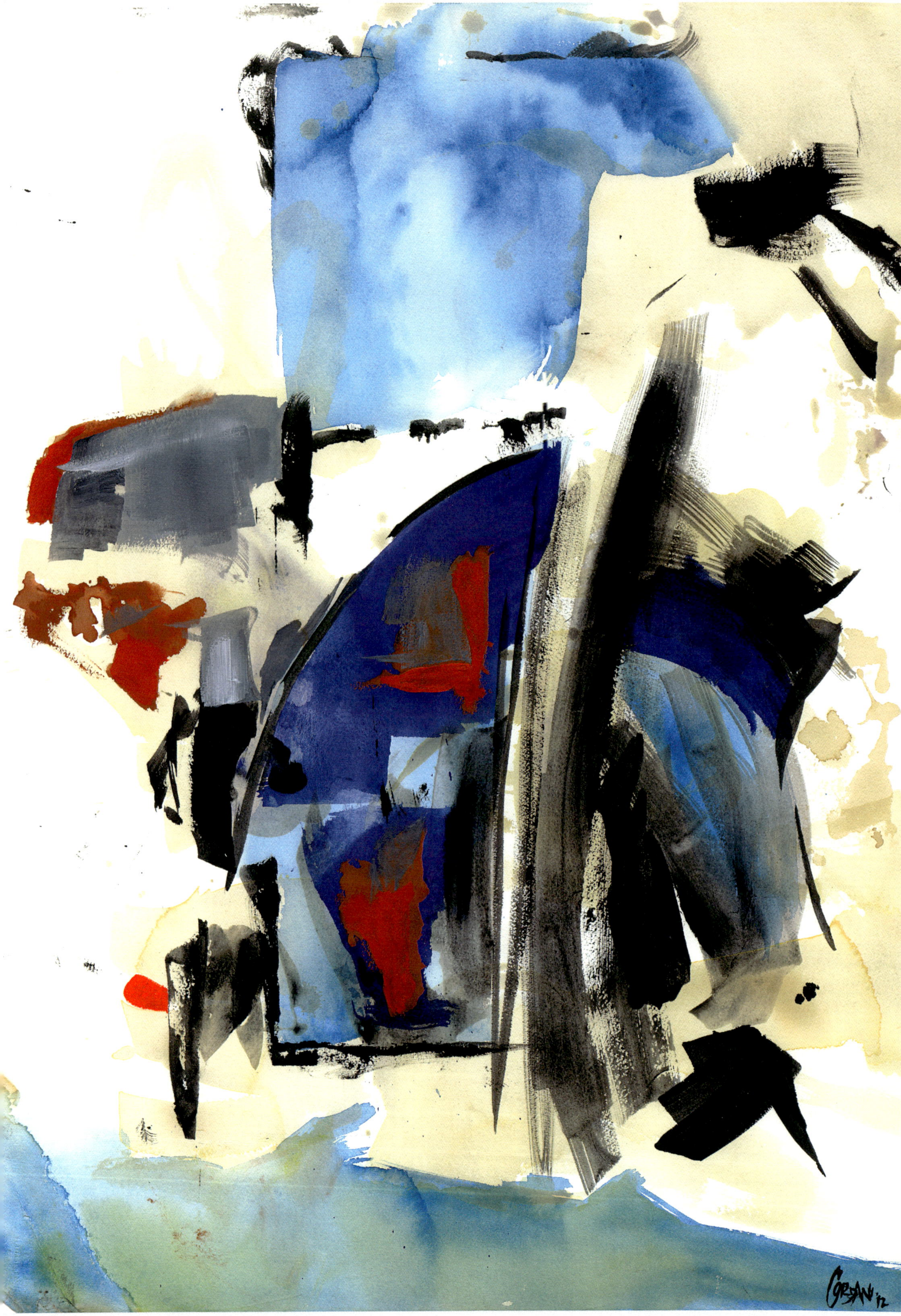

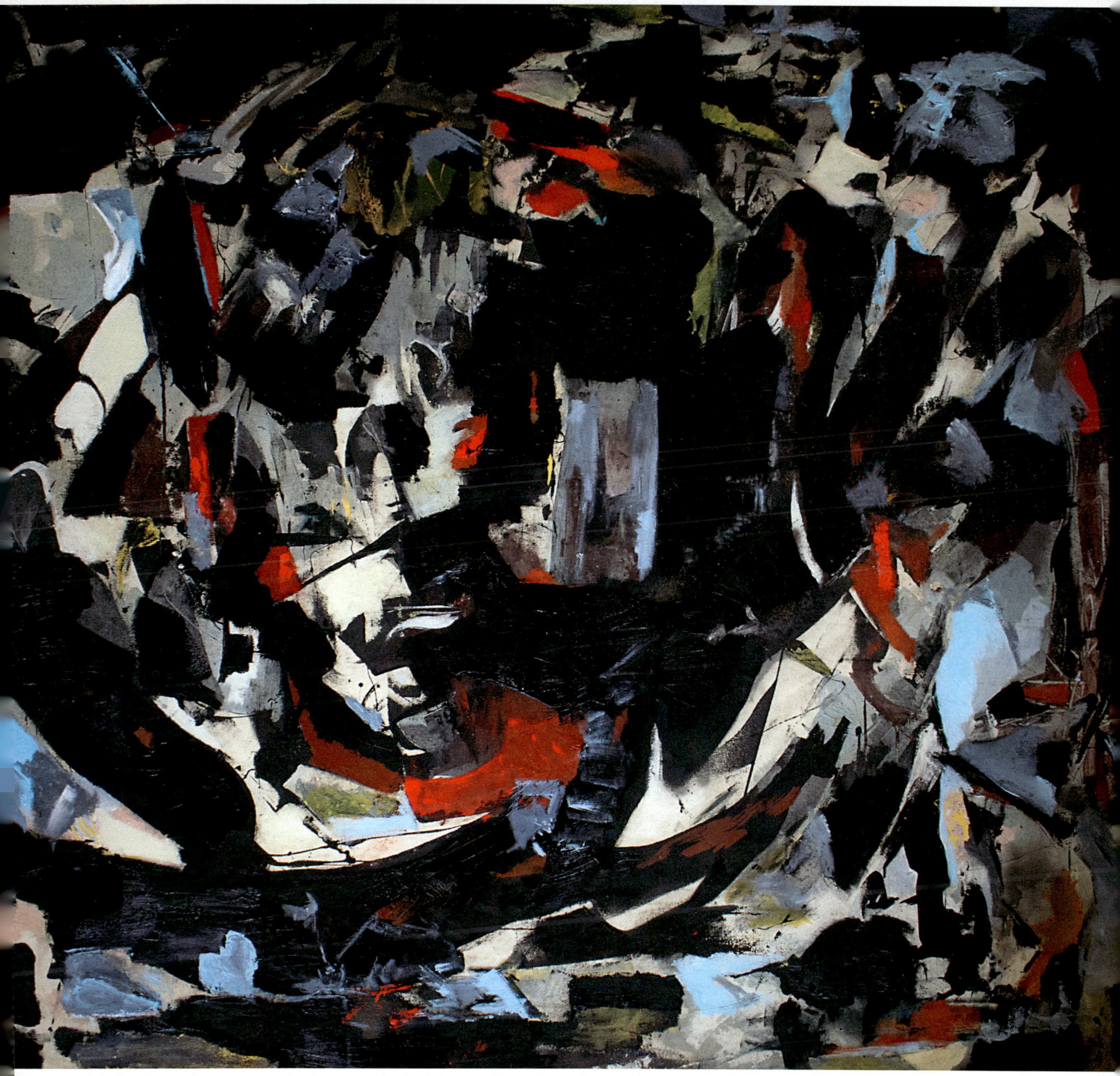

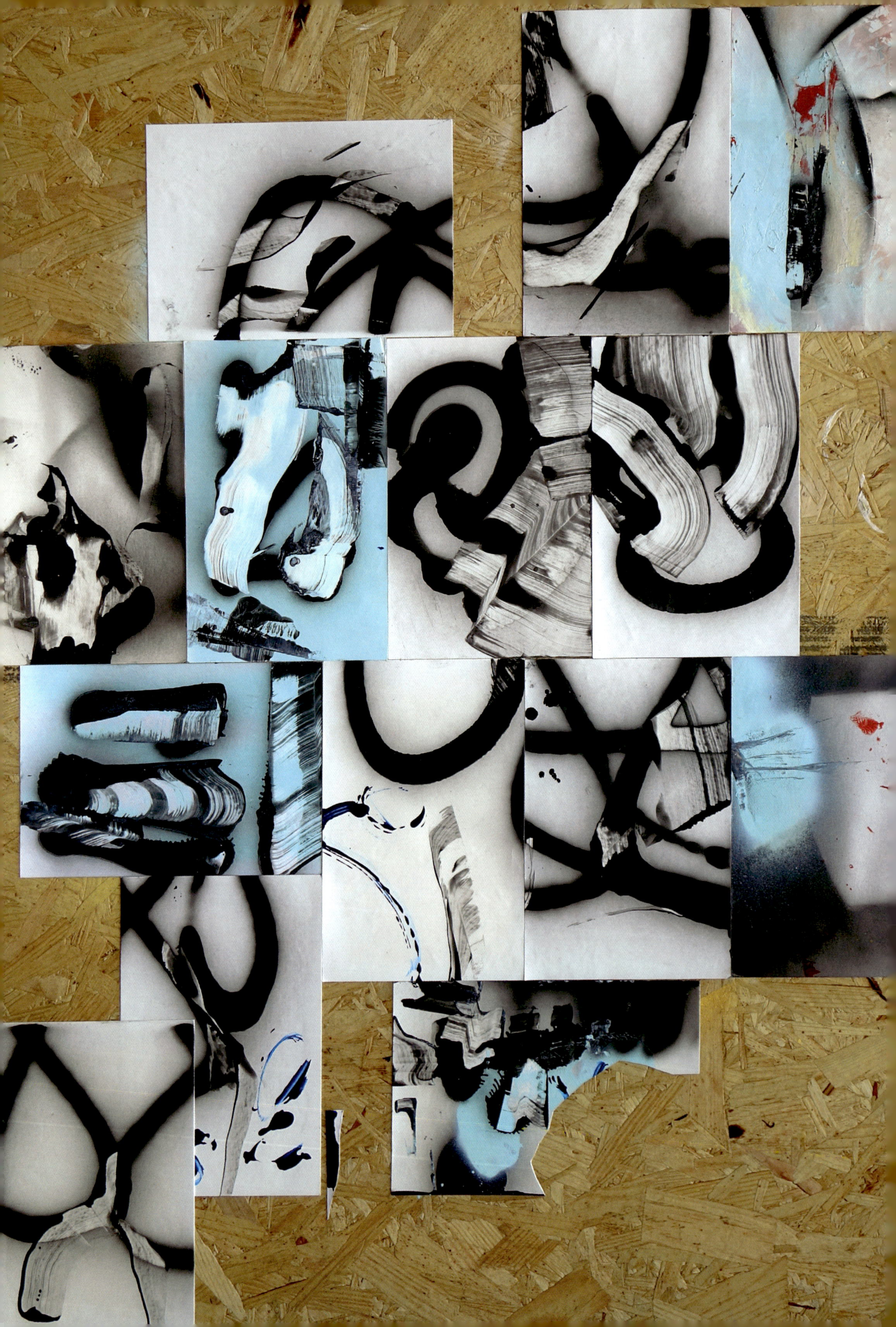

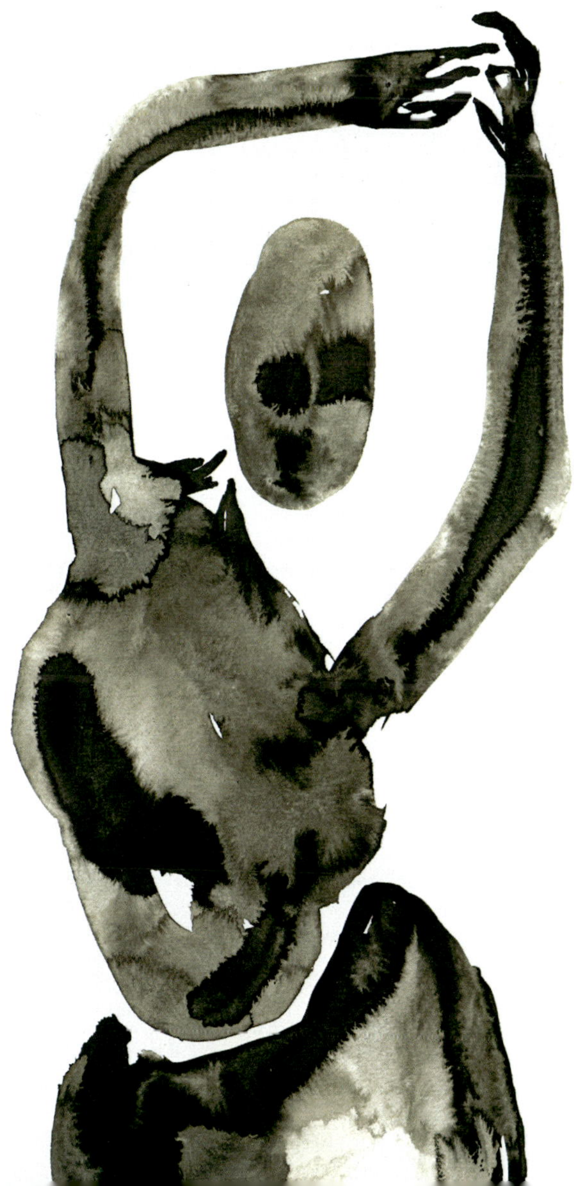

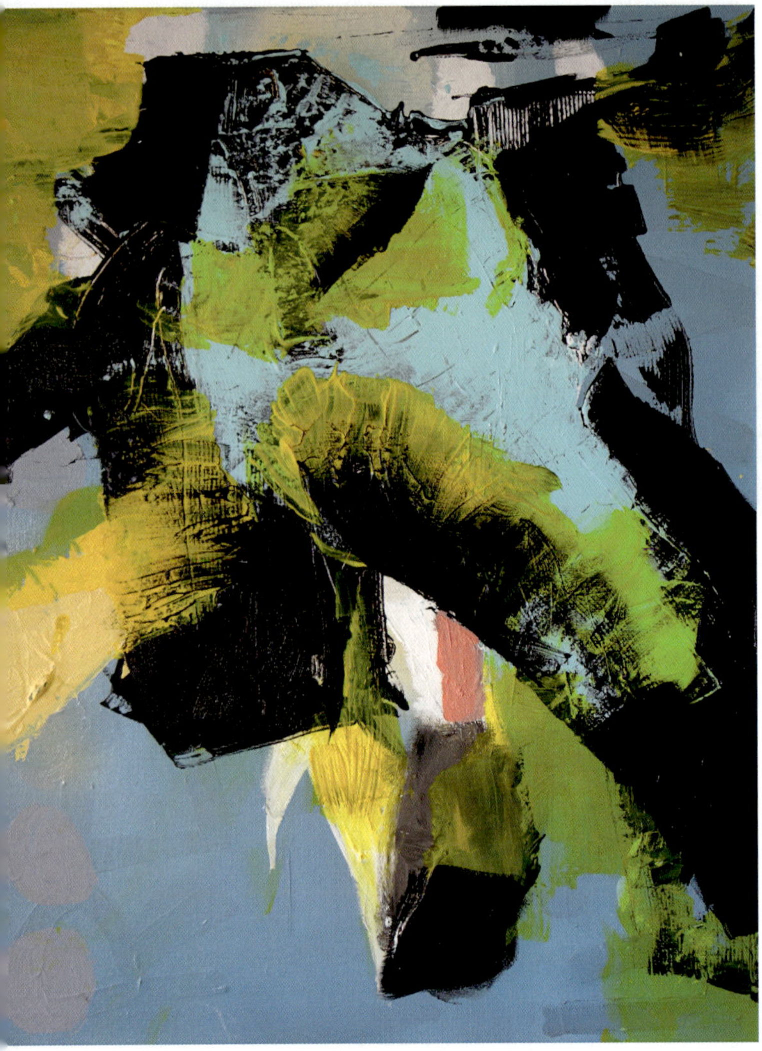

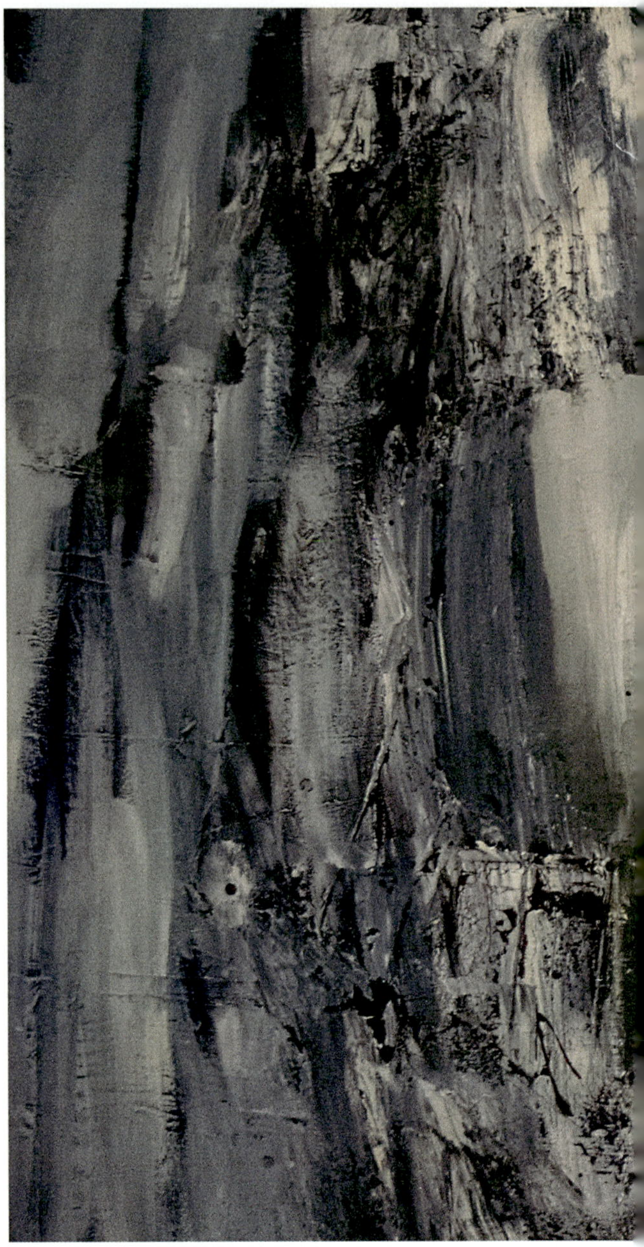

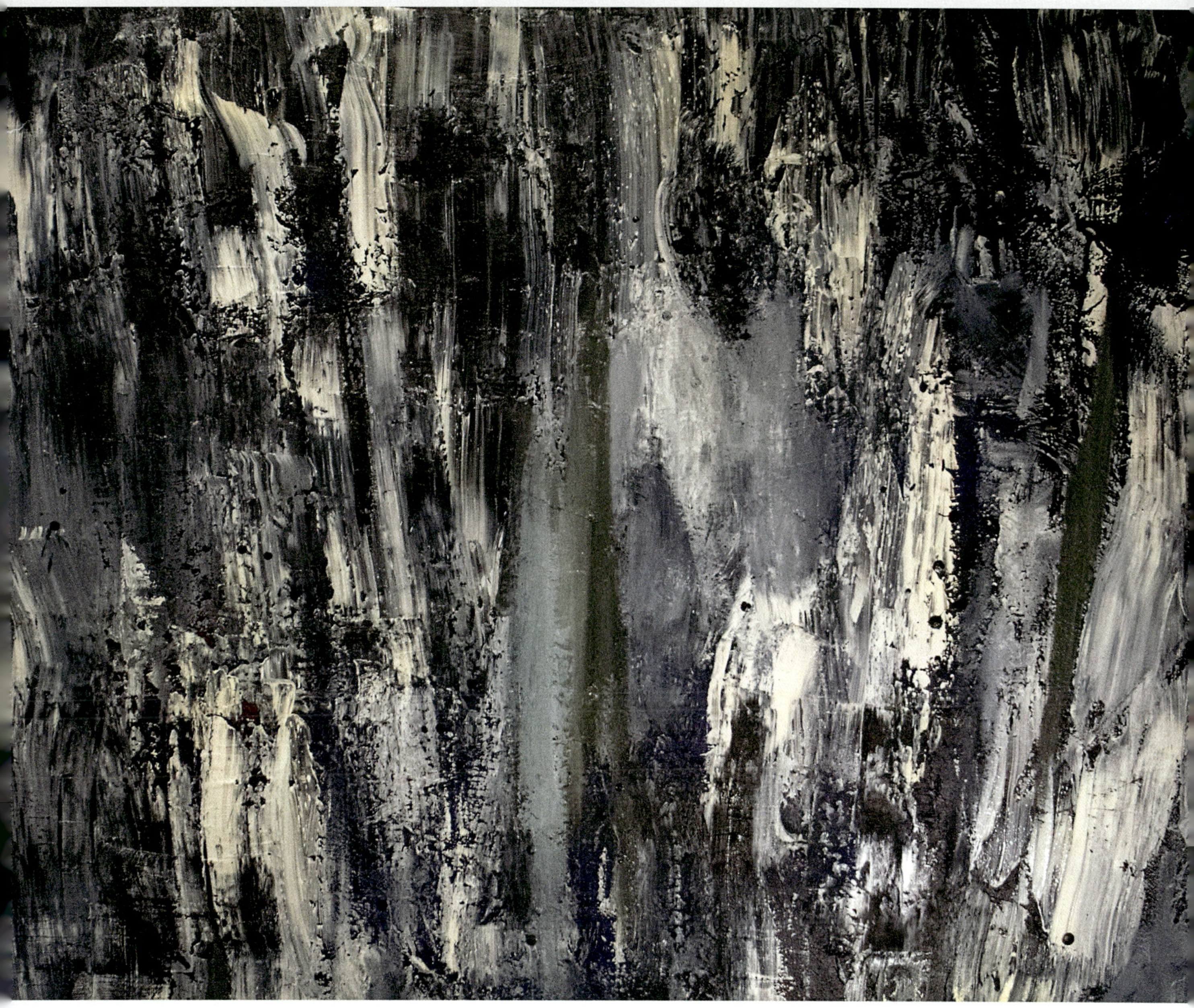

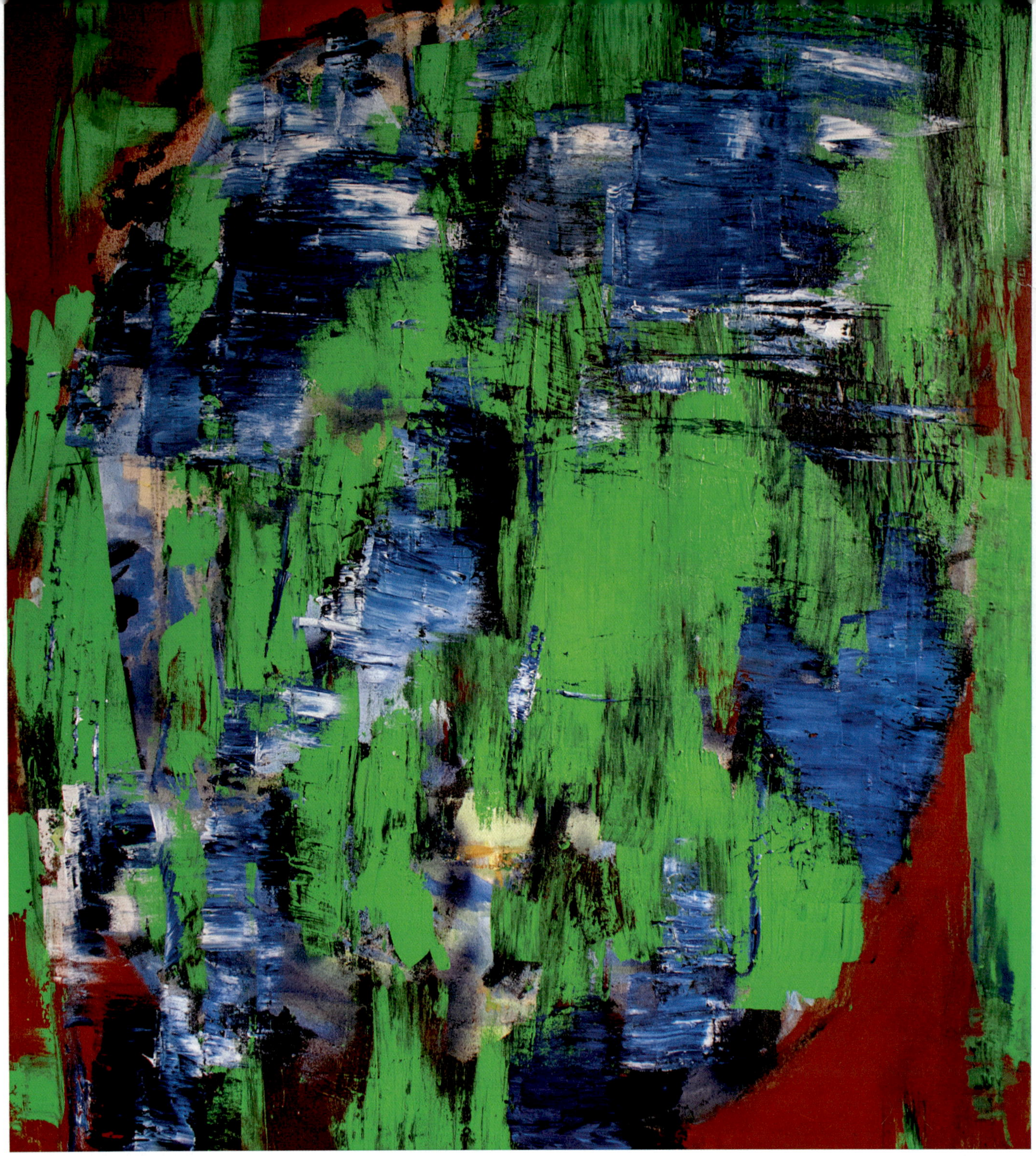

GRAVIDITY

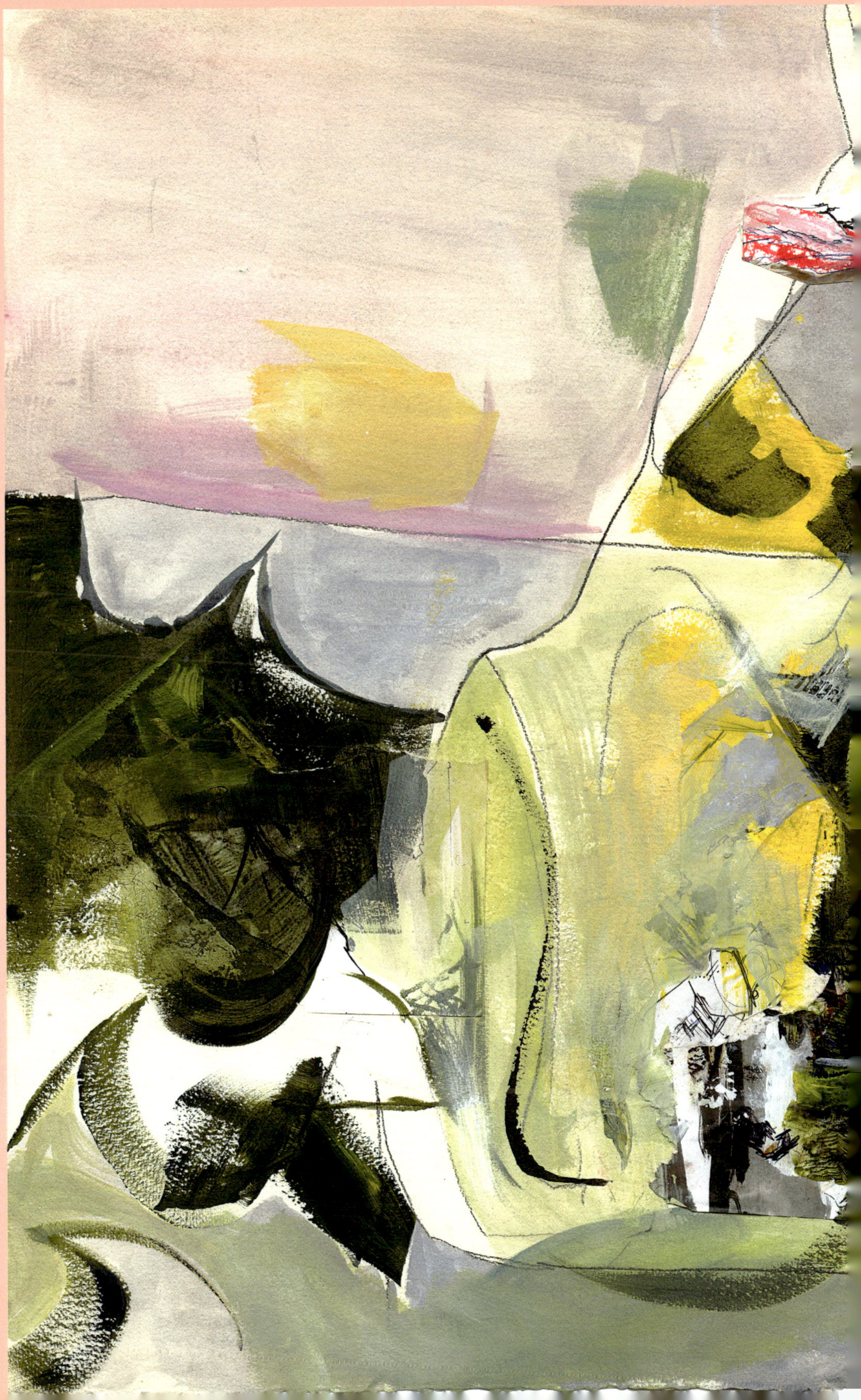

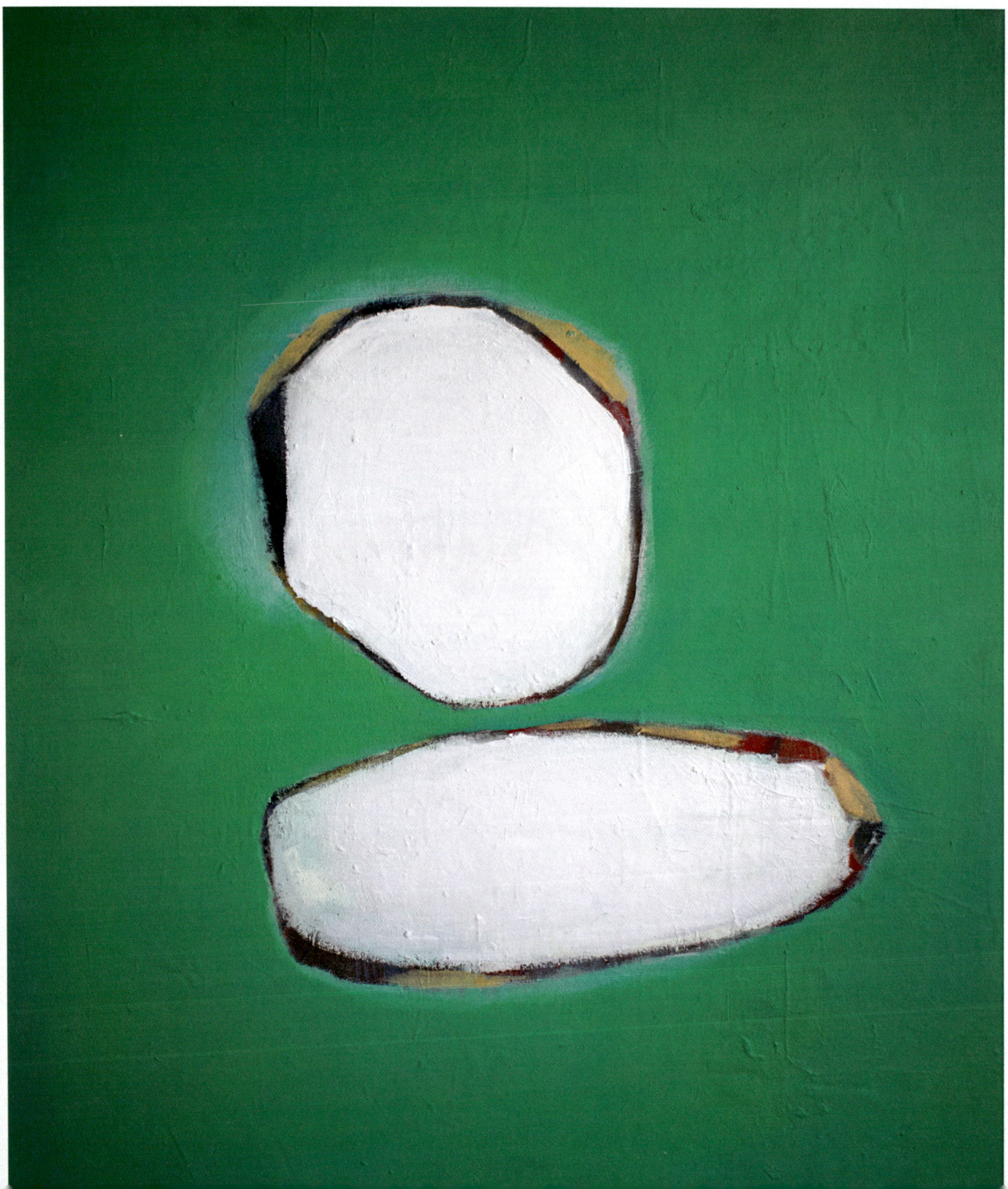

GRAVIDITY

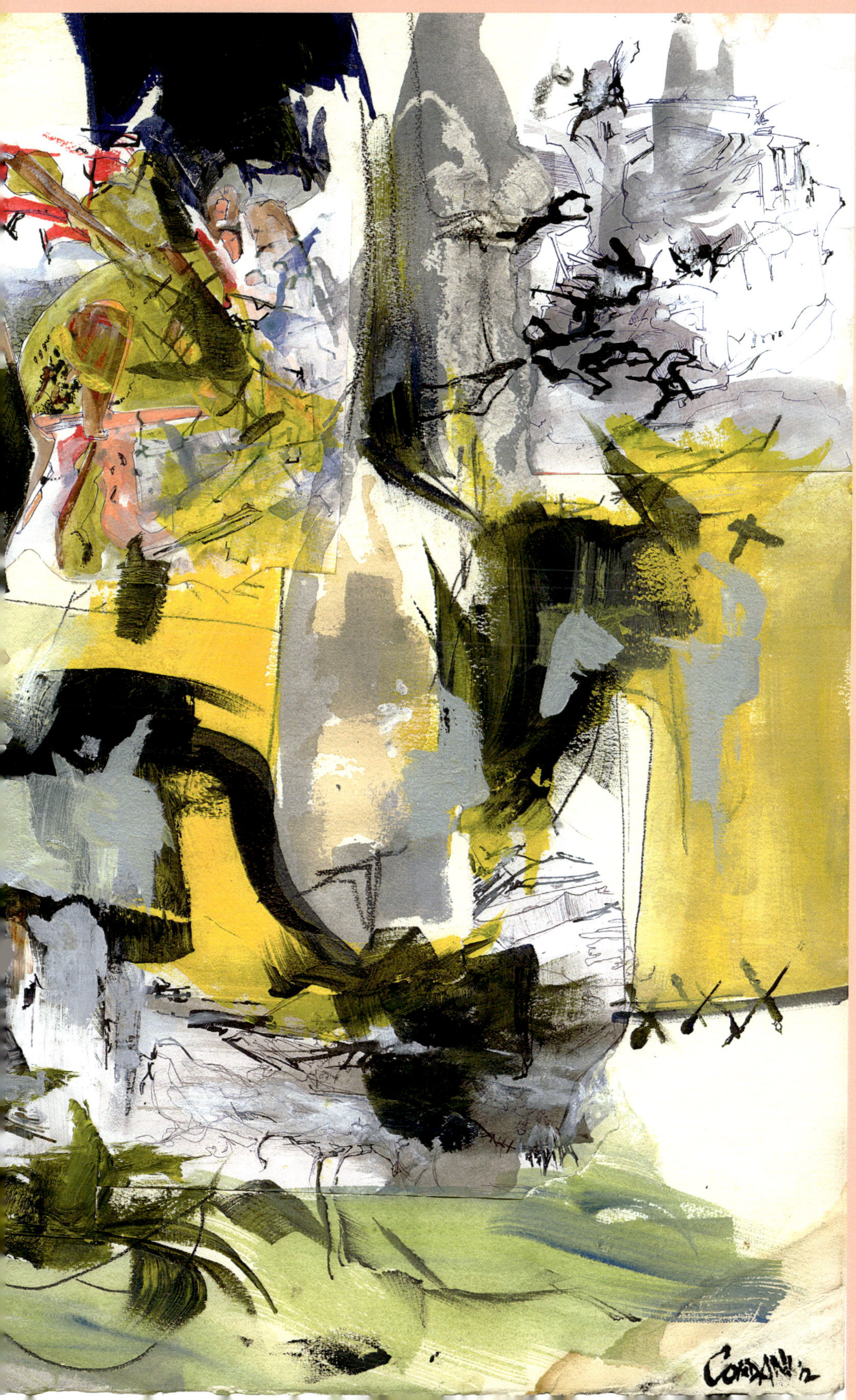

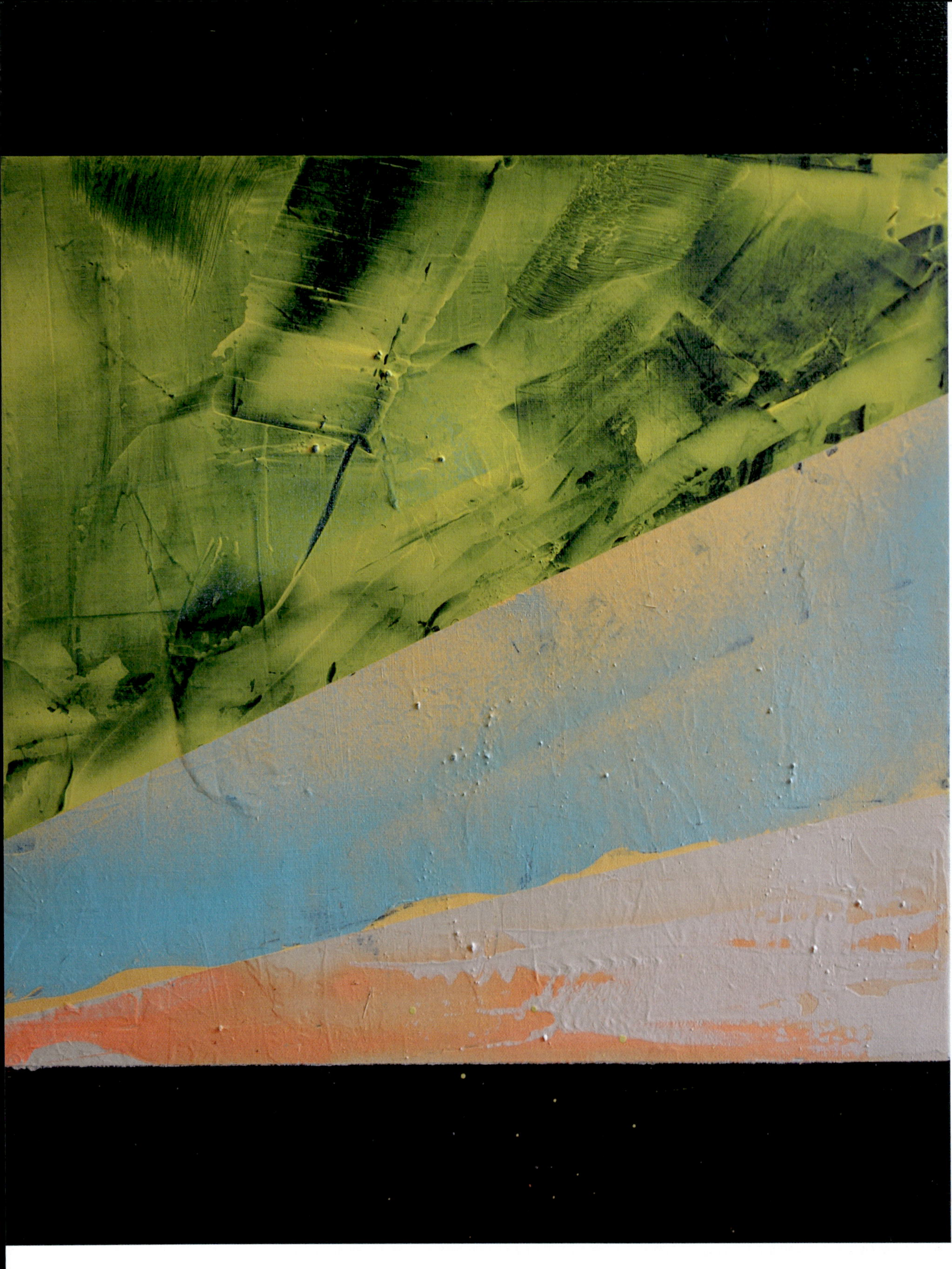

The challenge is

to say

I love you

without

using the words

I Love You

The challenge is

to say

I love you

without

using the words

I Love You

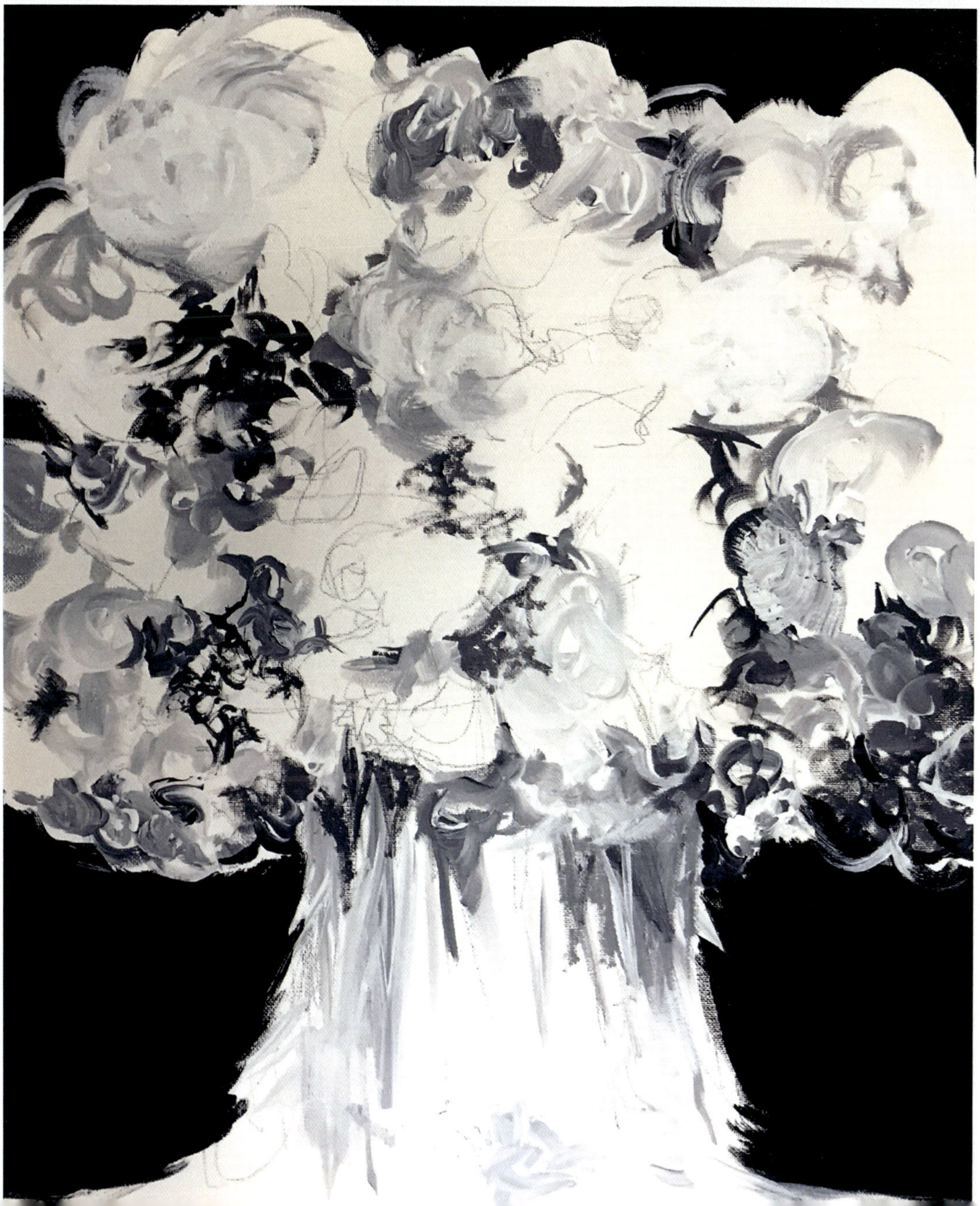

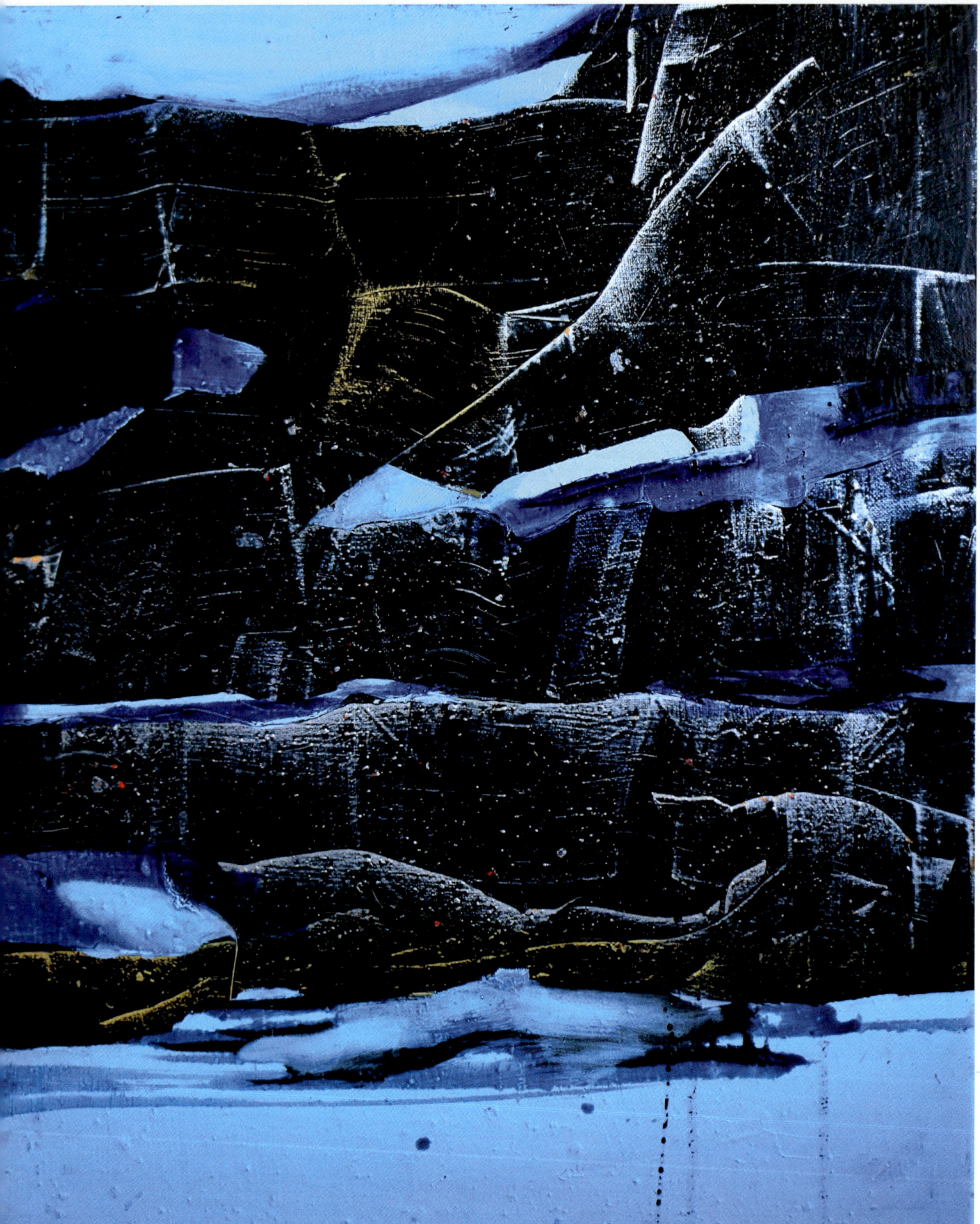

Marriage Naturalization
Citizenship

a permanent resident
is a character in
Dante's Inferno

Marriage Naturalization
Citizenship

a permanent resident
is a character in
Dante's Inferno

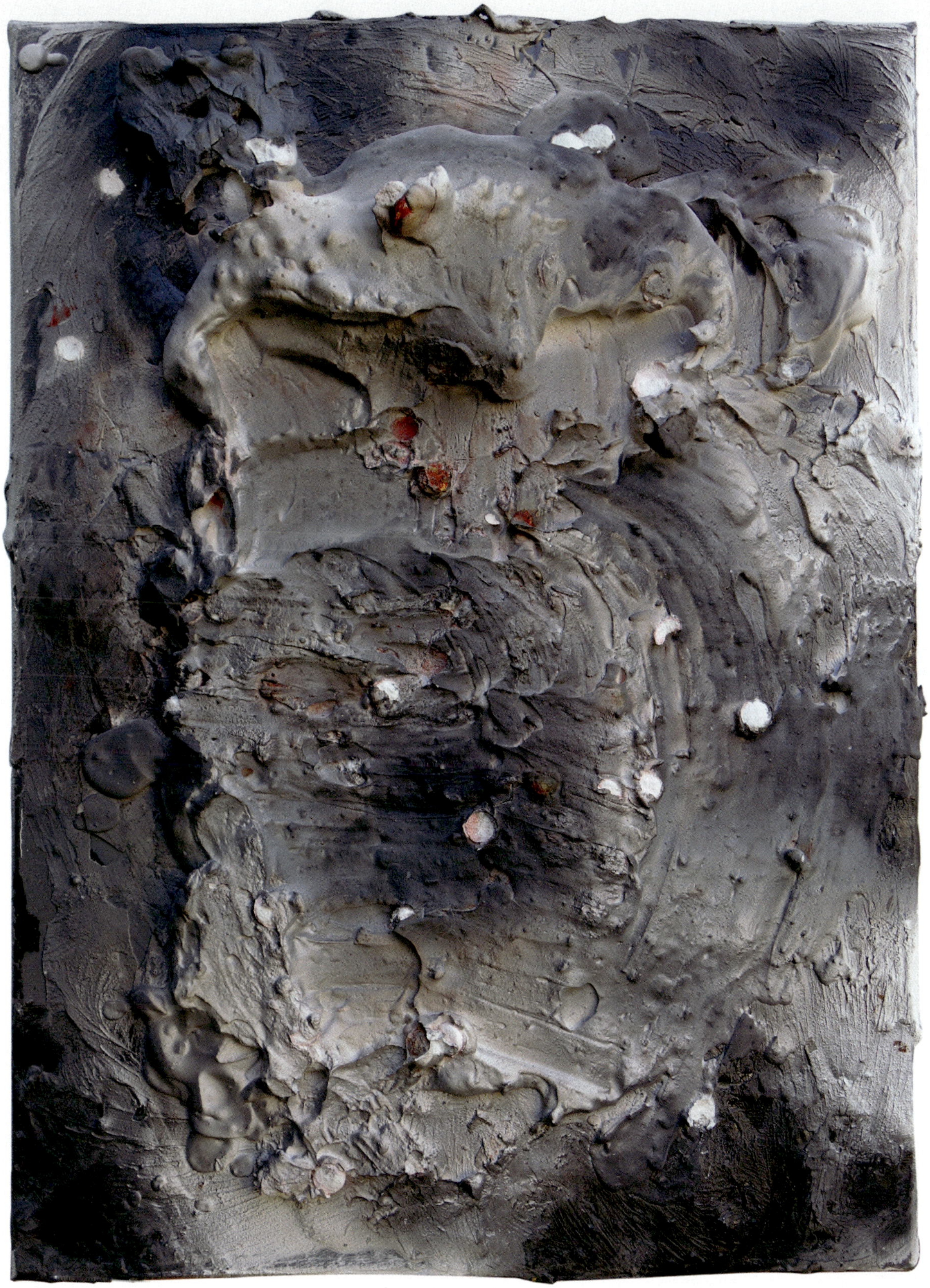

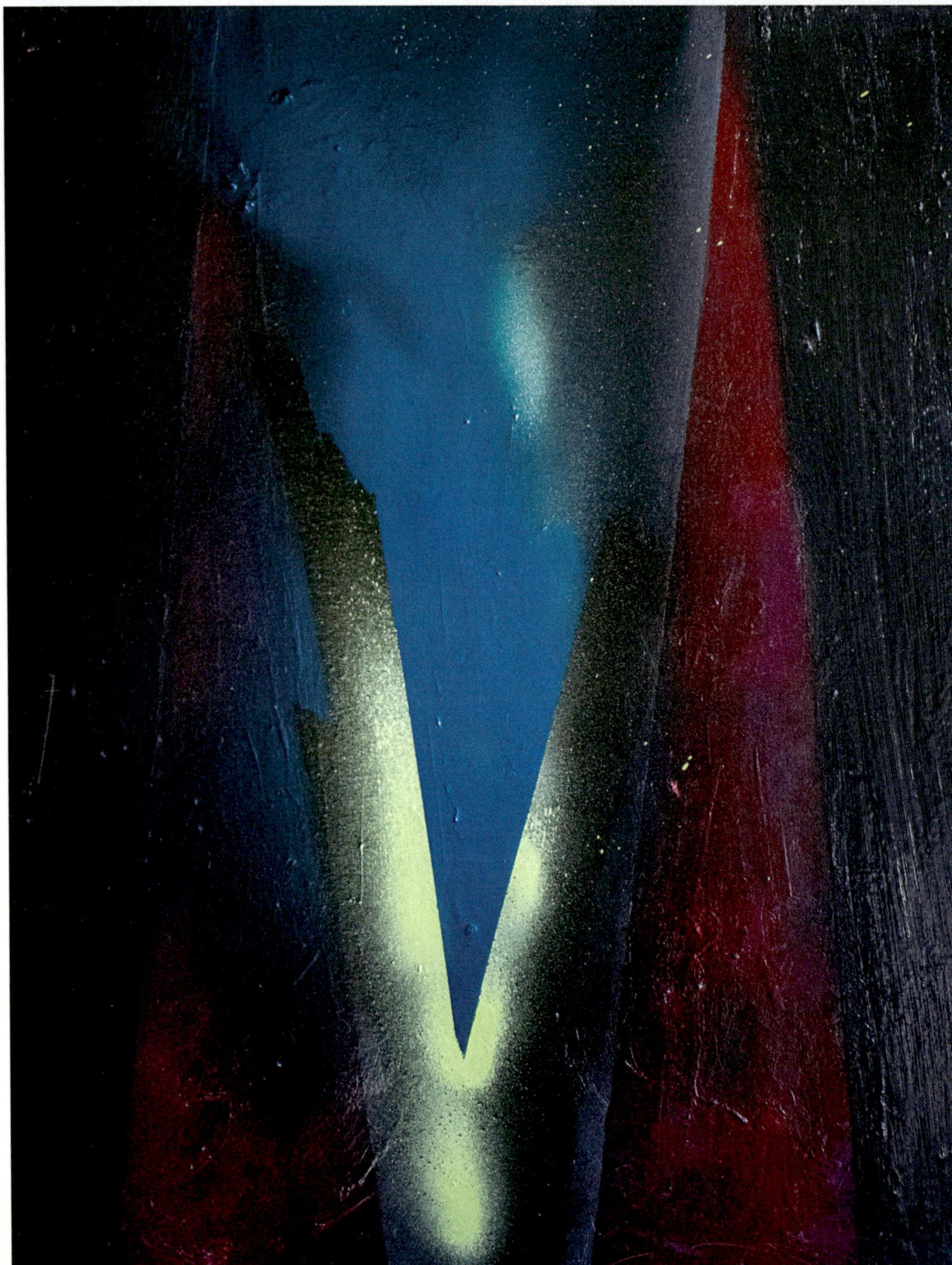

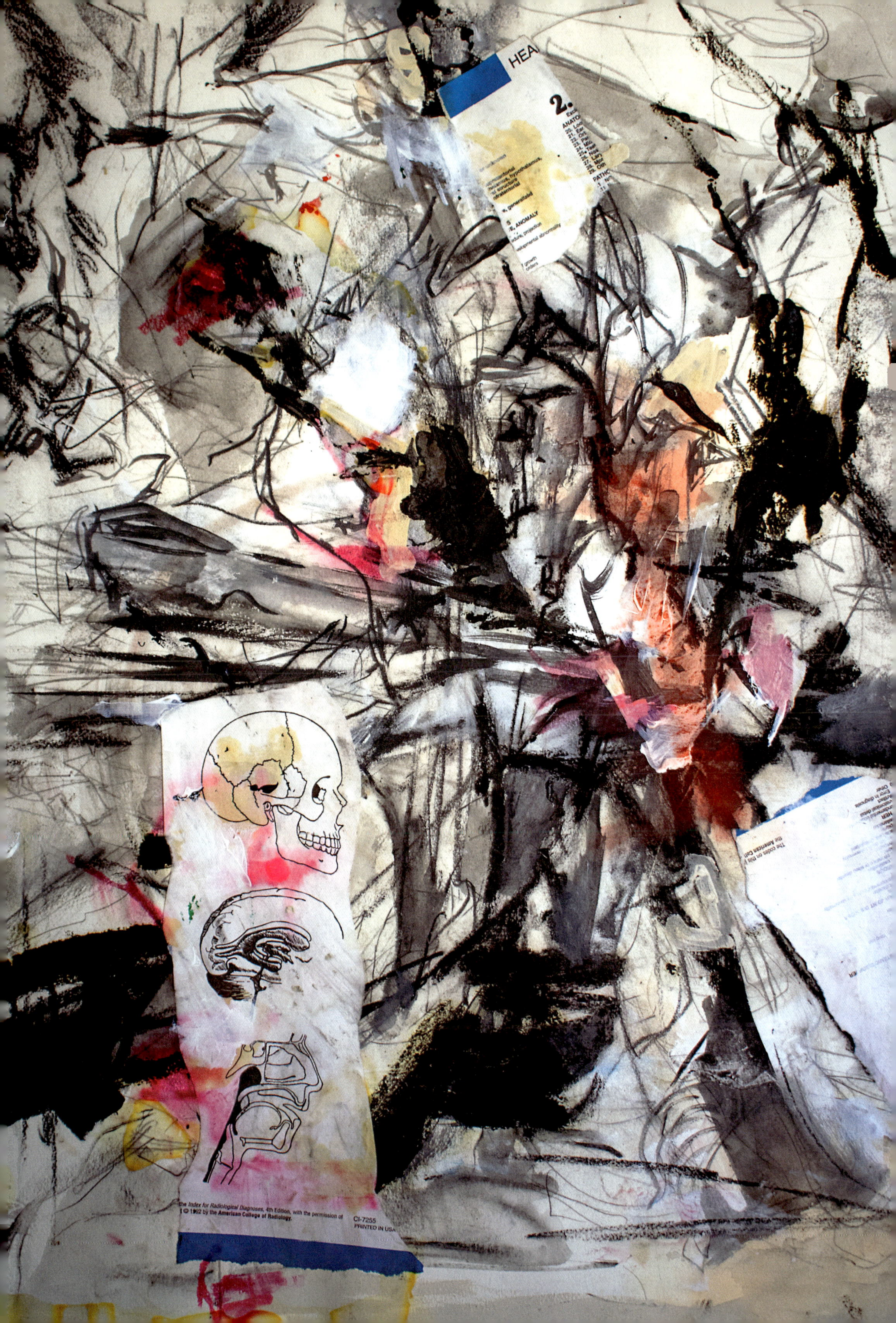
HEA
2.
the Index for Radiological Diagnoses, 4th Edition, with the permission of
© 1992 by the American College of Radiology.
CI-7255
PRINTED IN USA

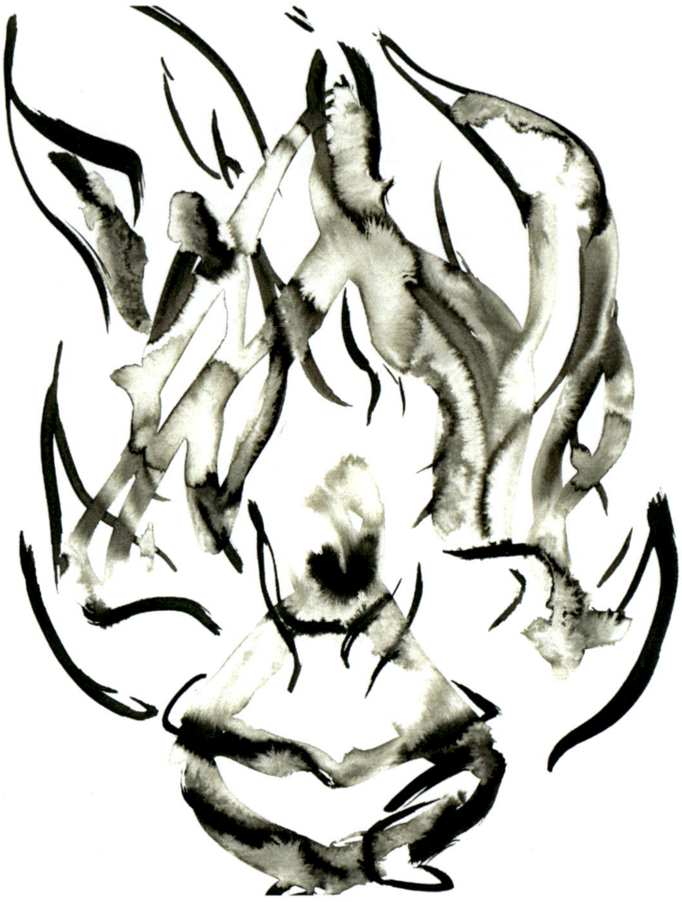

THE CELL

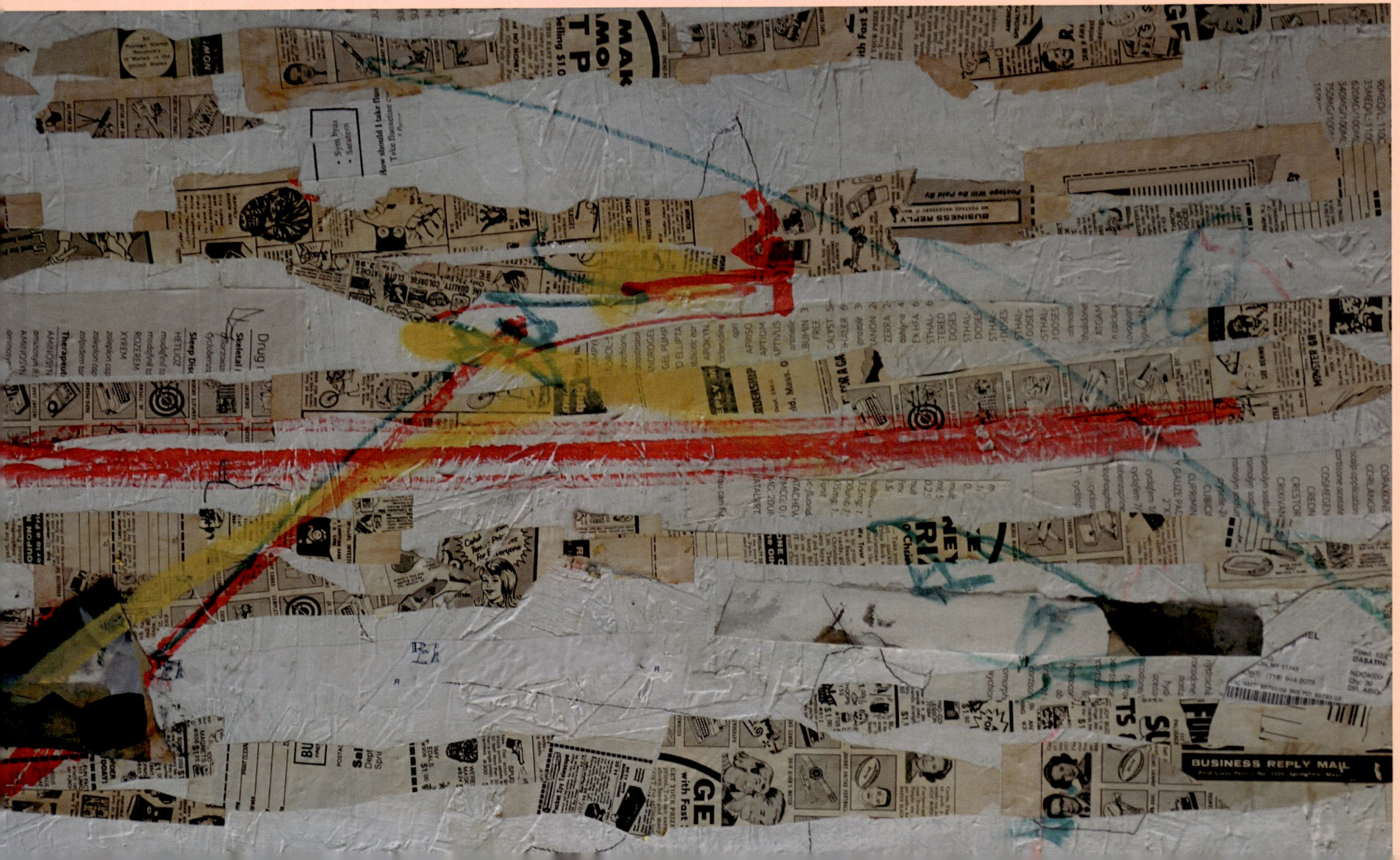

THE CELL

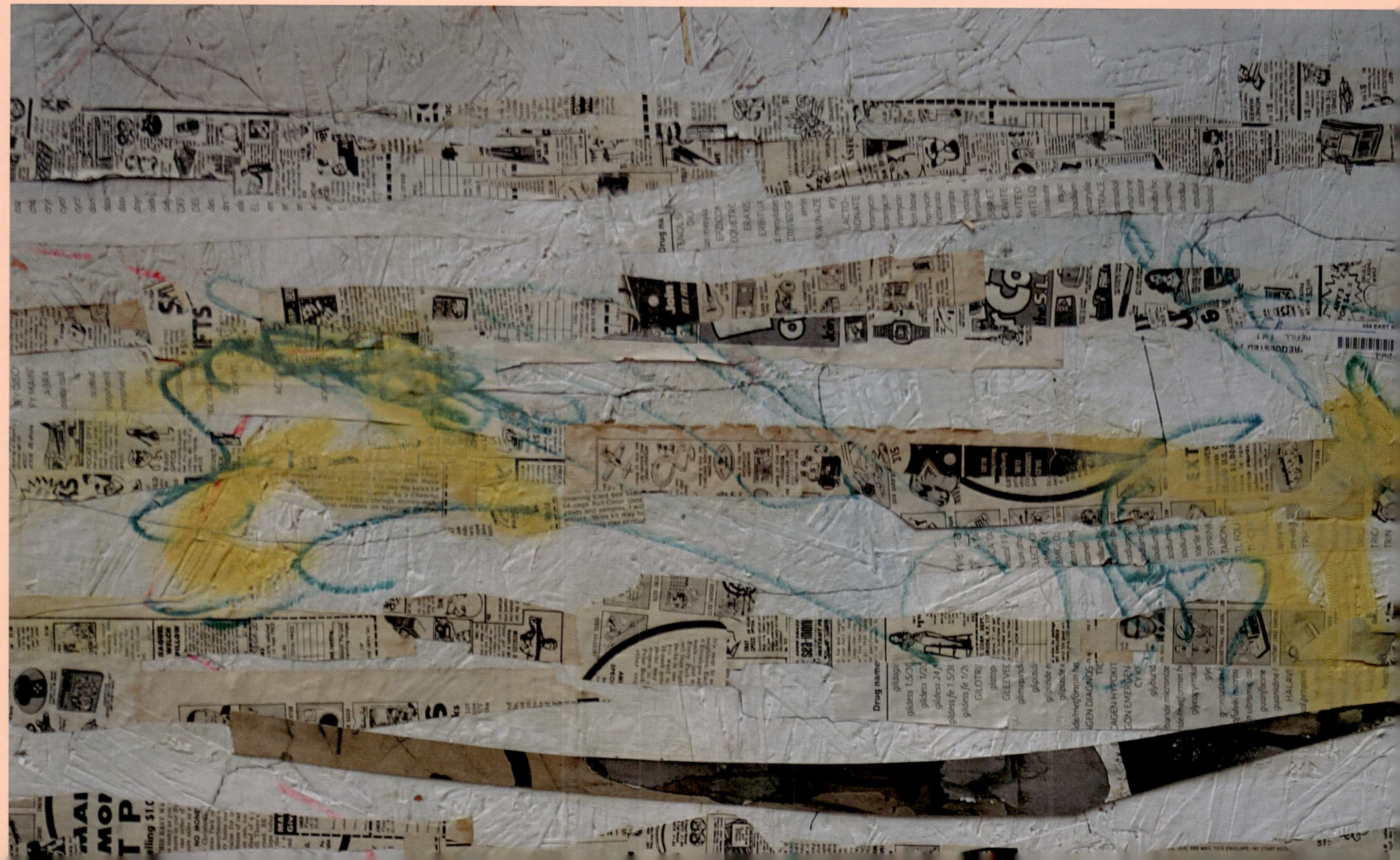

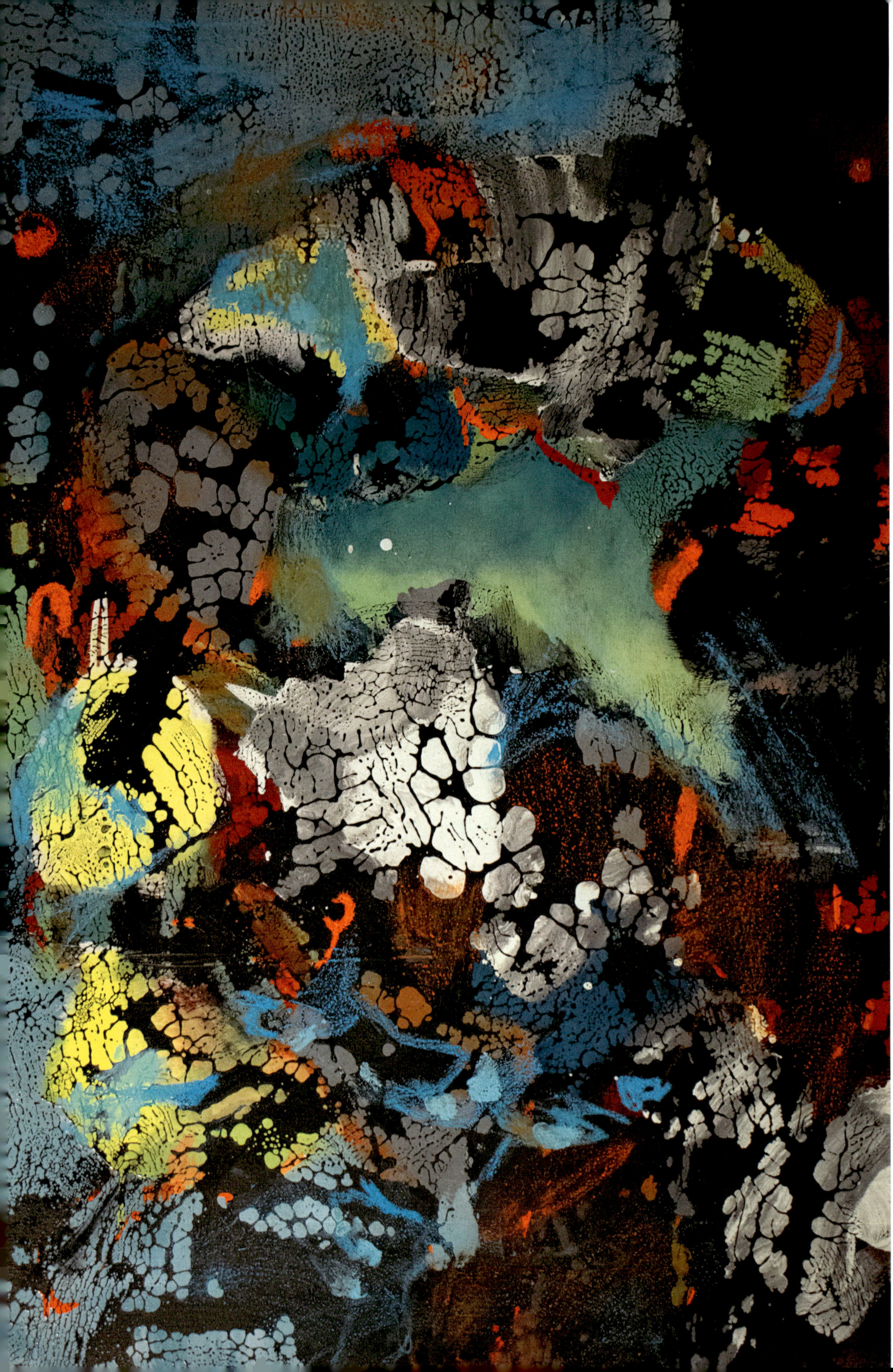

Here (I stick my hand
out the window) wind

Here (I put my hands
on my head) a cool
breeze

I'm a jazz man
Give me Monk
or Coltrane

Here (I stick my hand
out the window) wind

Here (I put my hands
on my head) a cool
breeze

I'm a jazz man
Give me Monk
or Coltrane

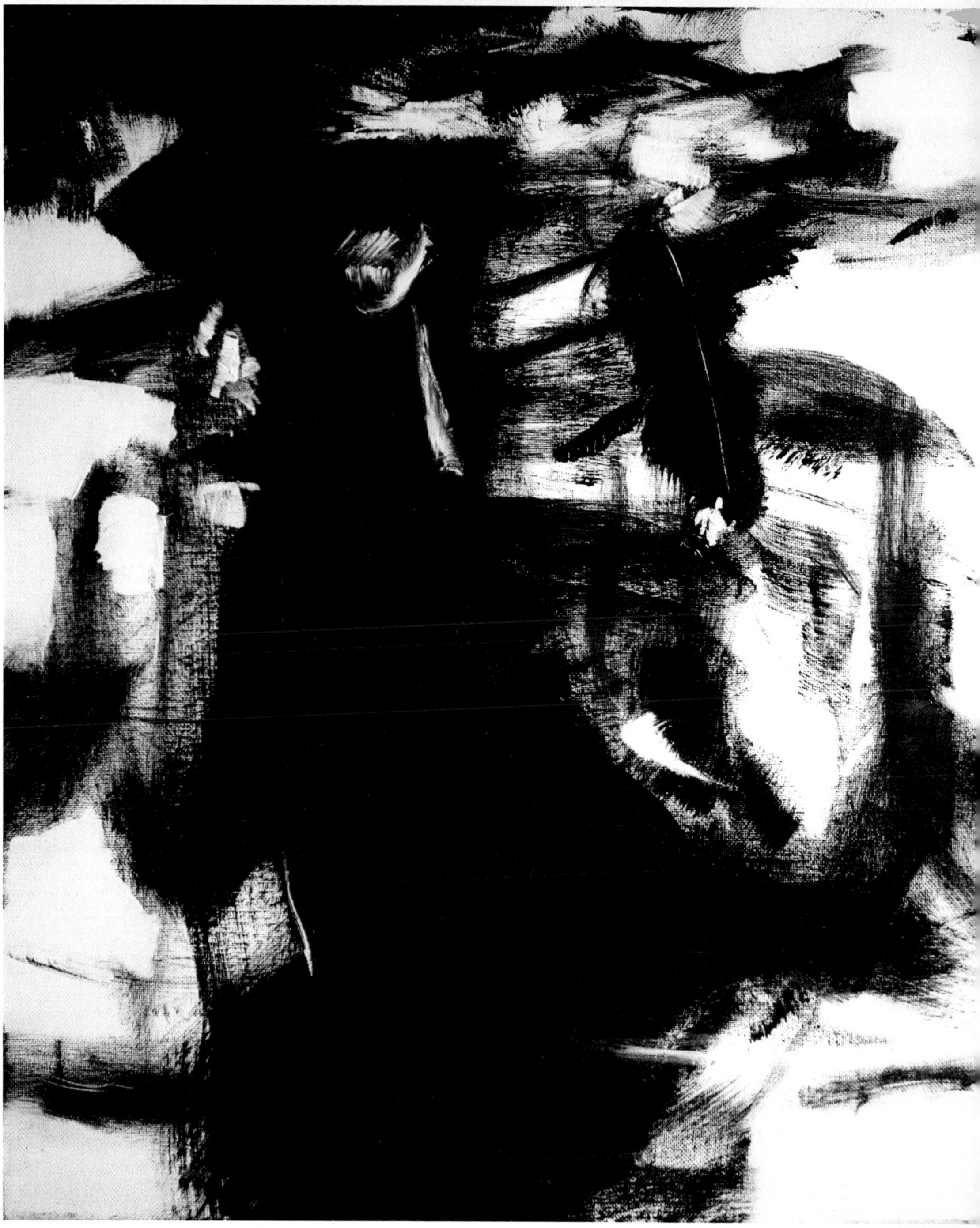

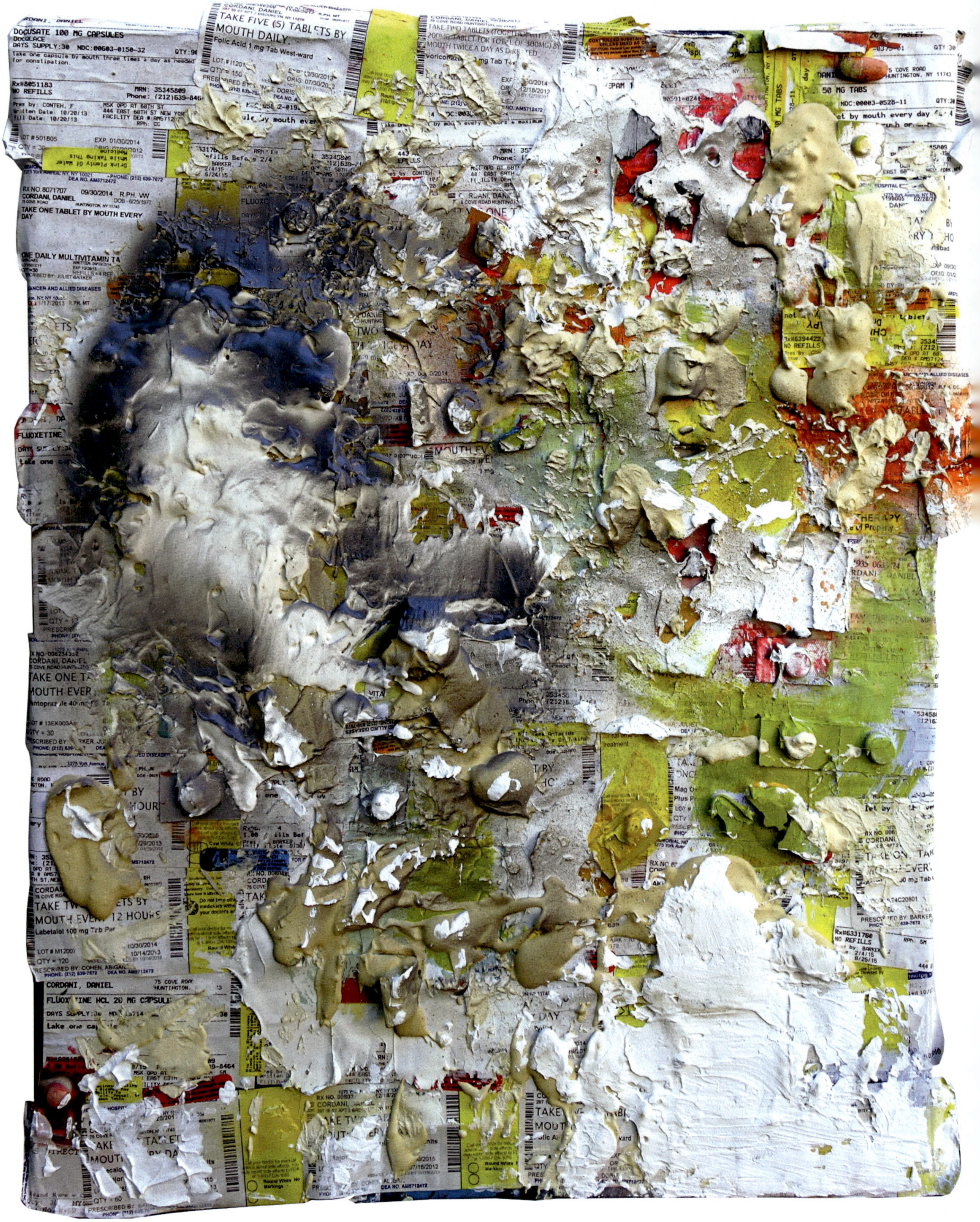
DOCUSATE 100 MG CAPSULES
TAKE FIVE (5) TABLETS BY
MOUTH DAILY
Folic Acid 1 mg Tab West-ward
NO REFILLS
TAKE ONE TABLET BY MOUTH EVERY DAY
ONE DAILY MULTIVITAMIN TA
FLUOXETINE
50 MG TABS
CORDANI, DANIEL

The world
is my rival

I'm deprived
of innocence

The world
is my rival

I'm deprived
of innocence

*Then is
it nothing
for you
to be
in jail?*

*It is
the curtain
in a theater*

Then is
it nothing
for you
to be
in jail?

It is
the curtain
in a theater

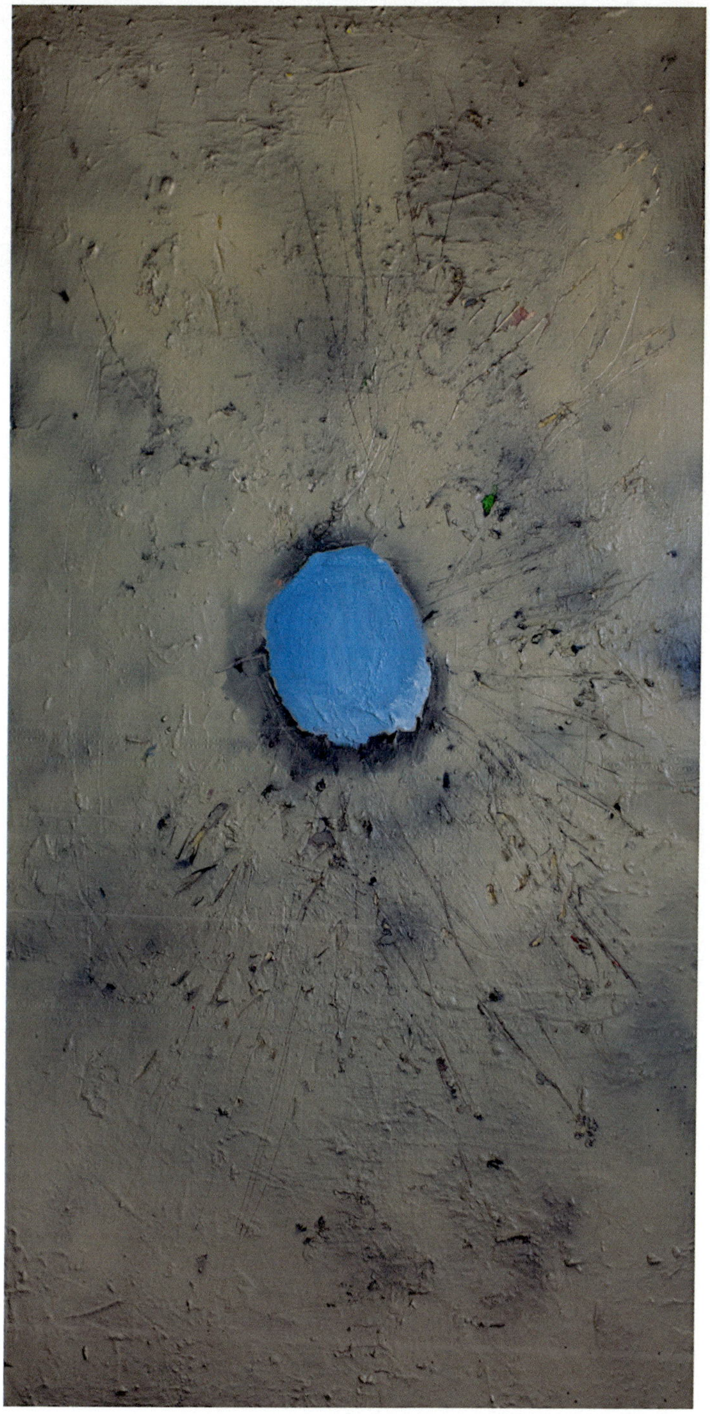

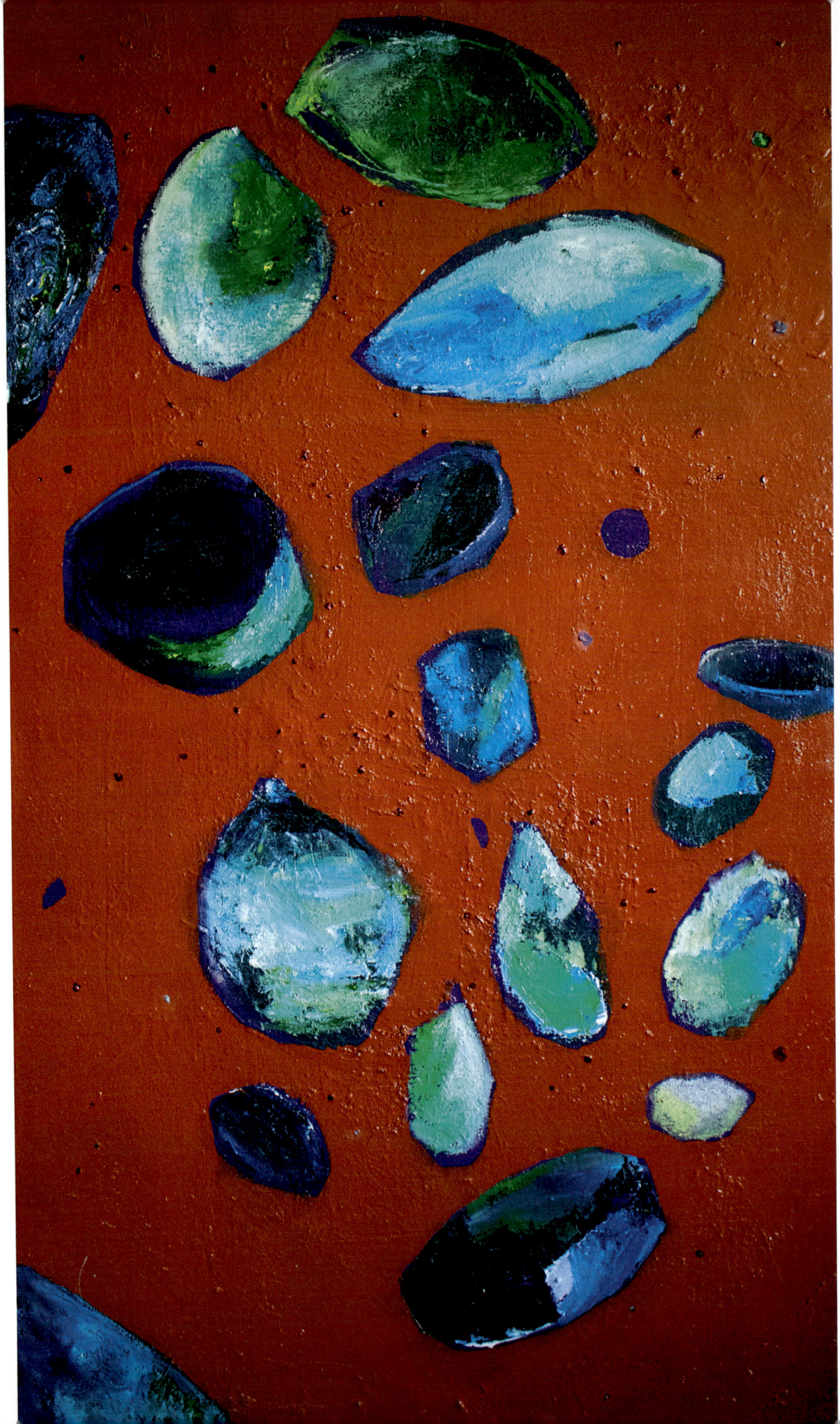

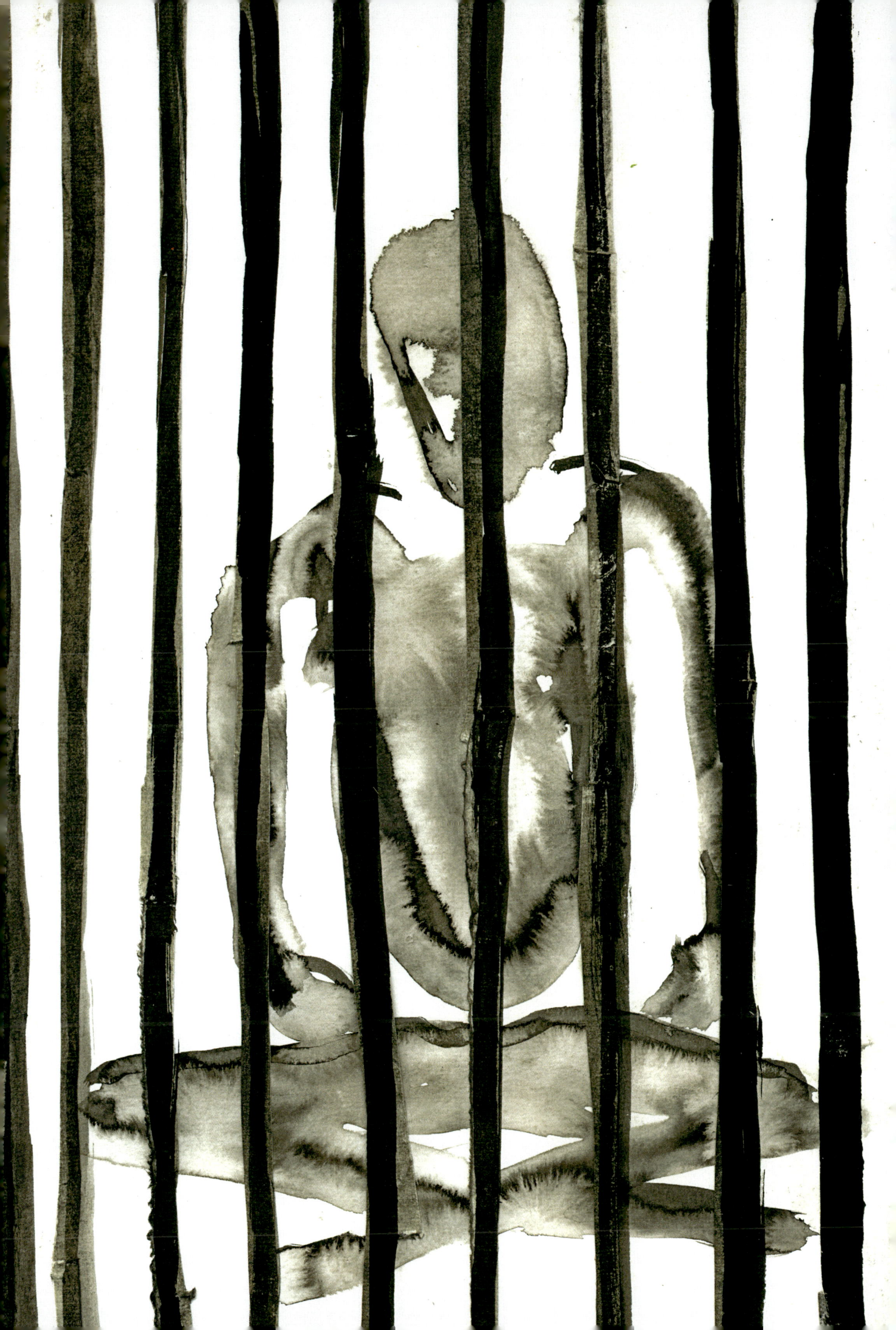

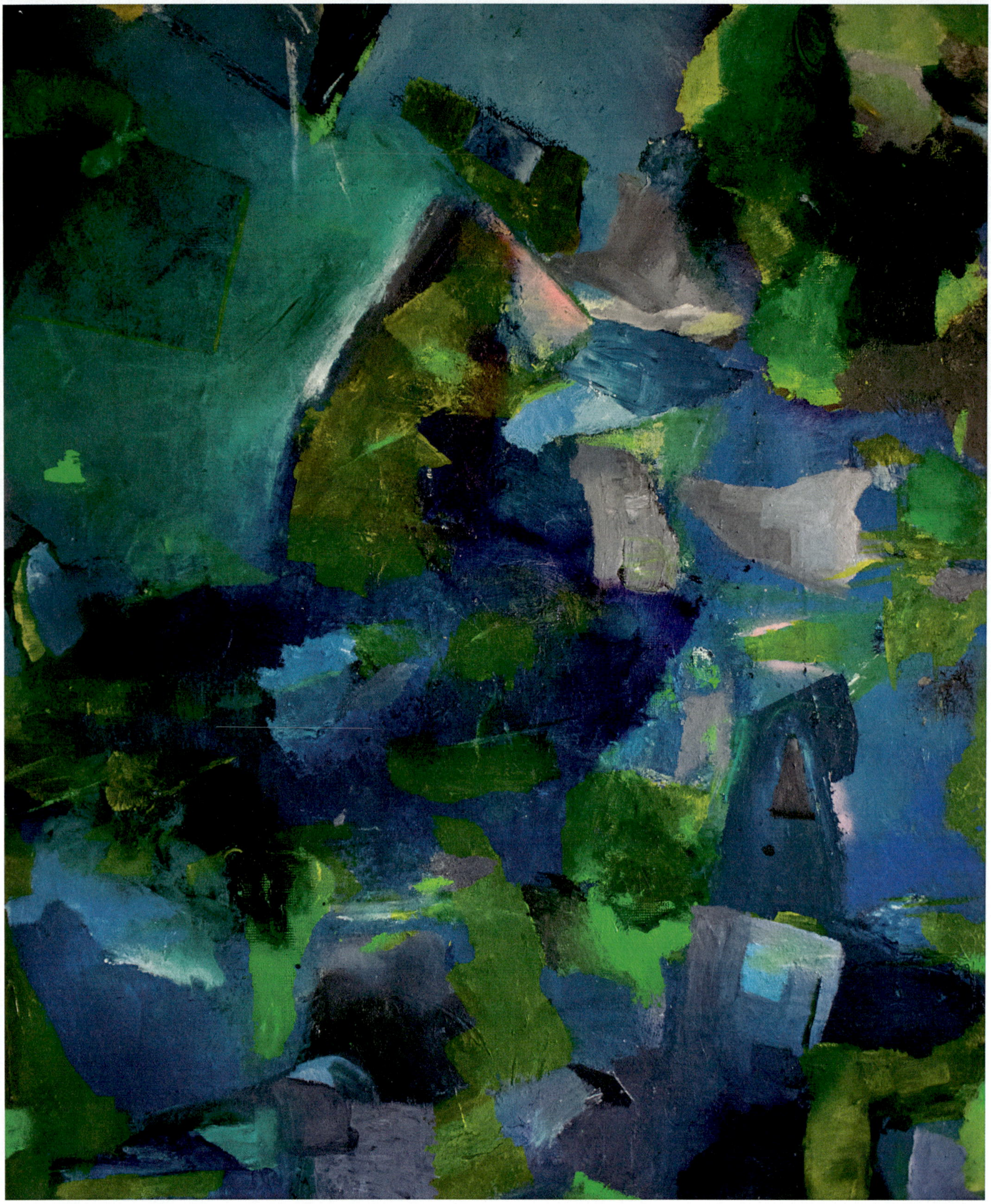

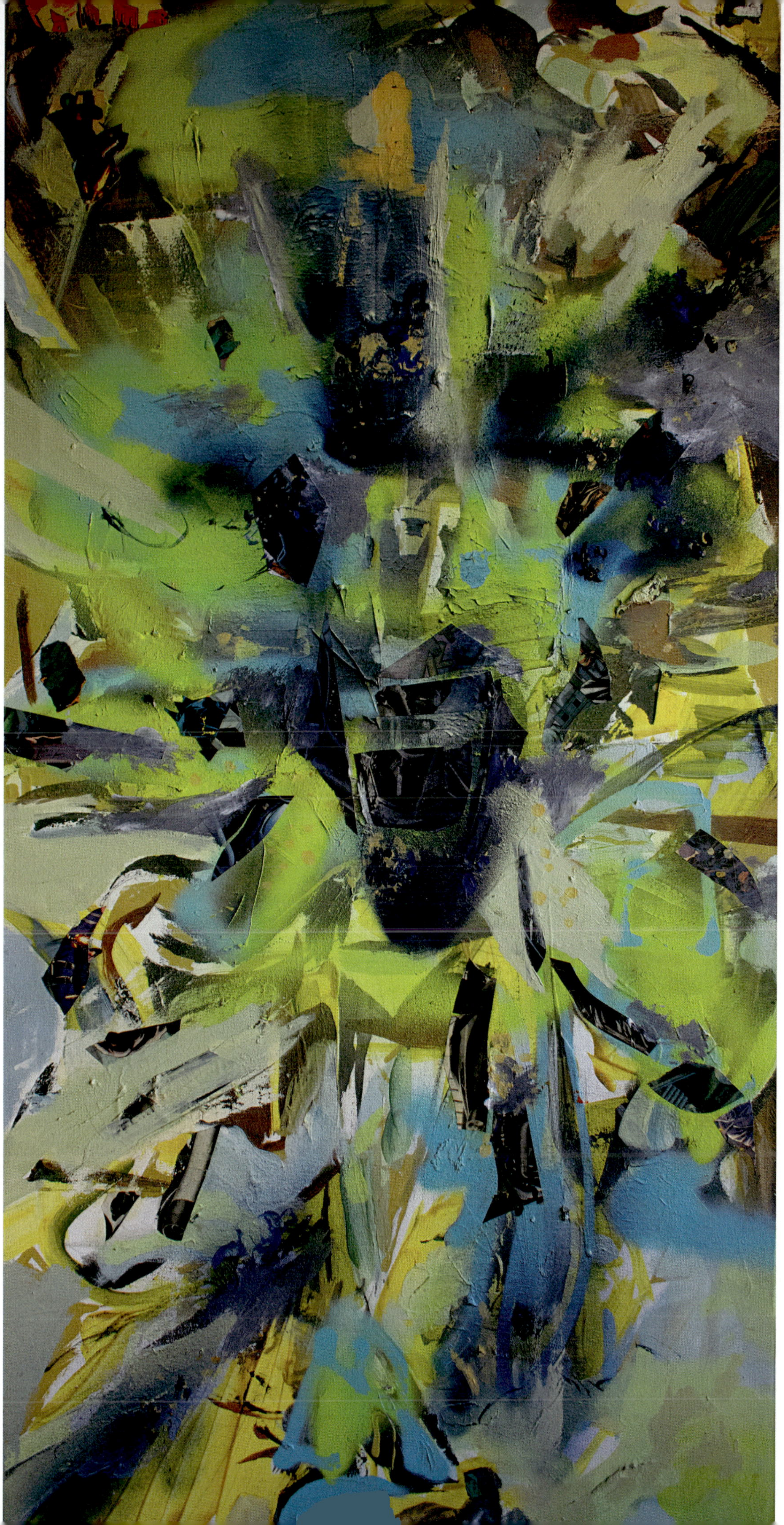

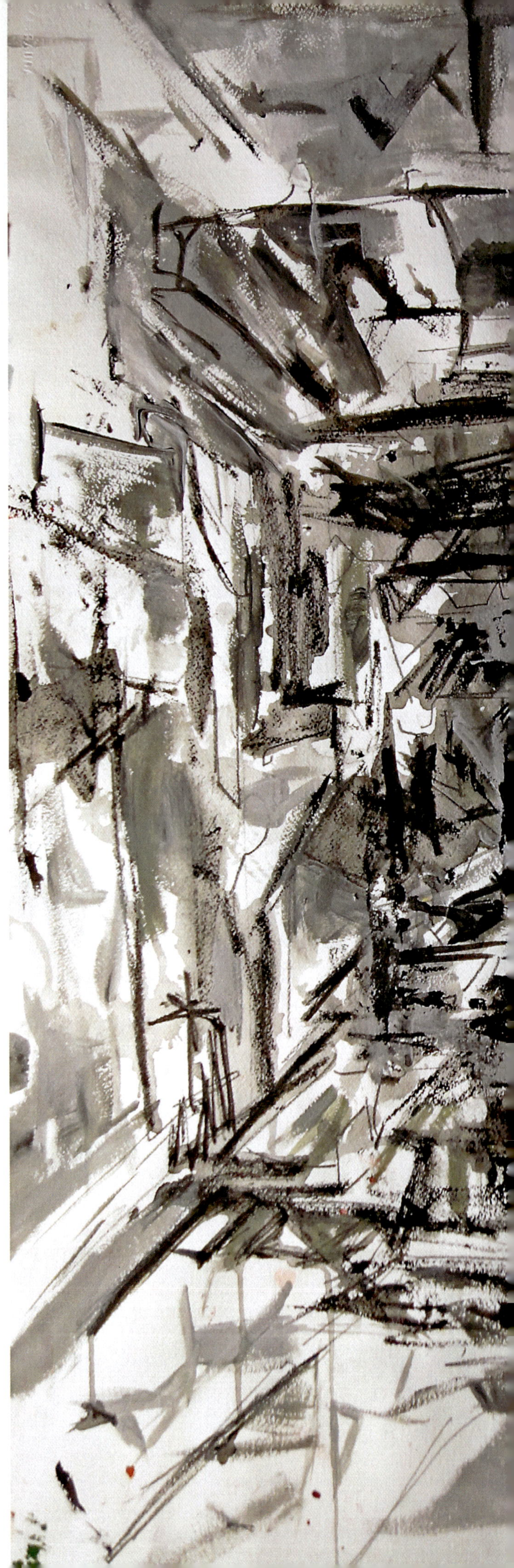

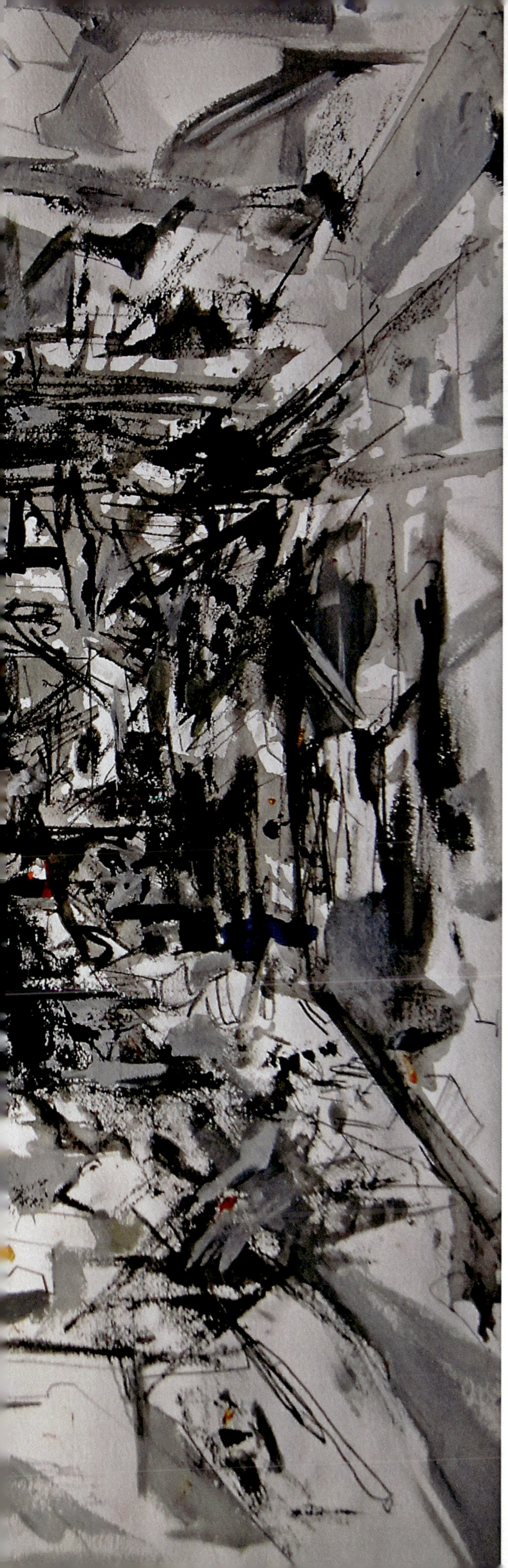

TRUMP NOW

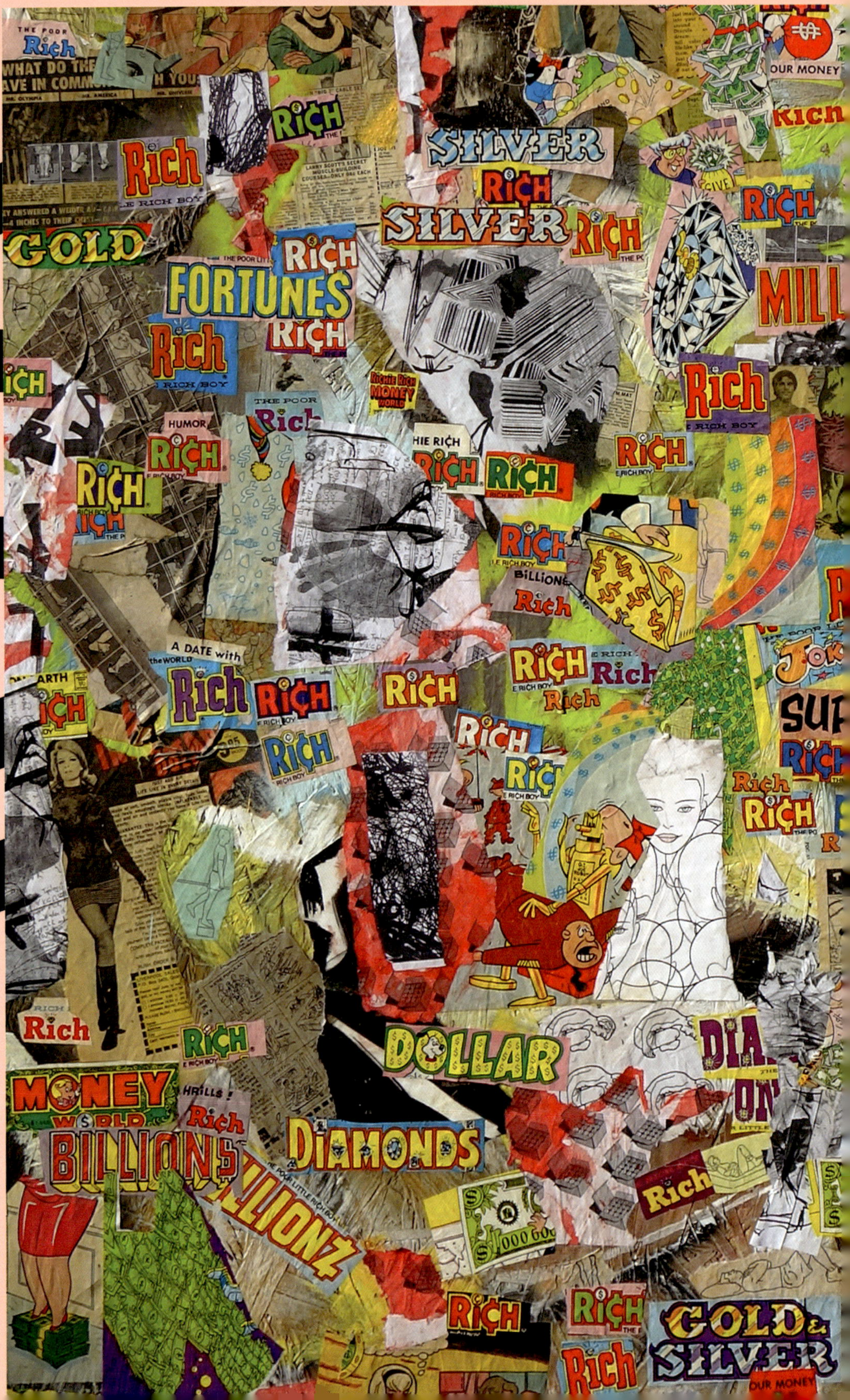
SILVER
GOLD
FORTUNES
Rich
DOLLAR
DIAMONDS
MONEY
BILLIONS
GOLD & SILVER

TRUMP WON

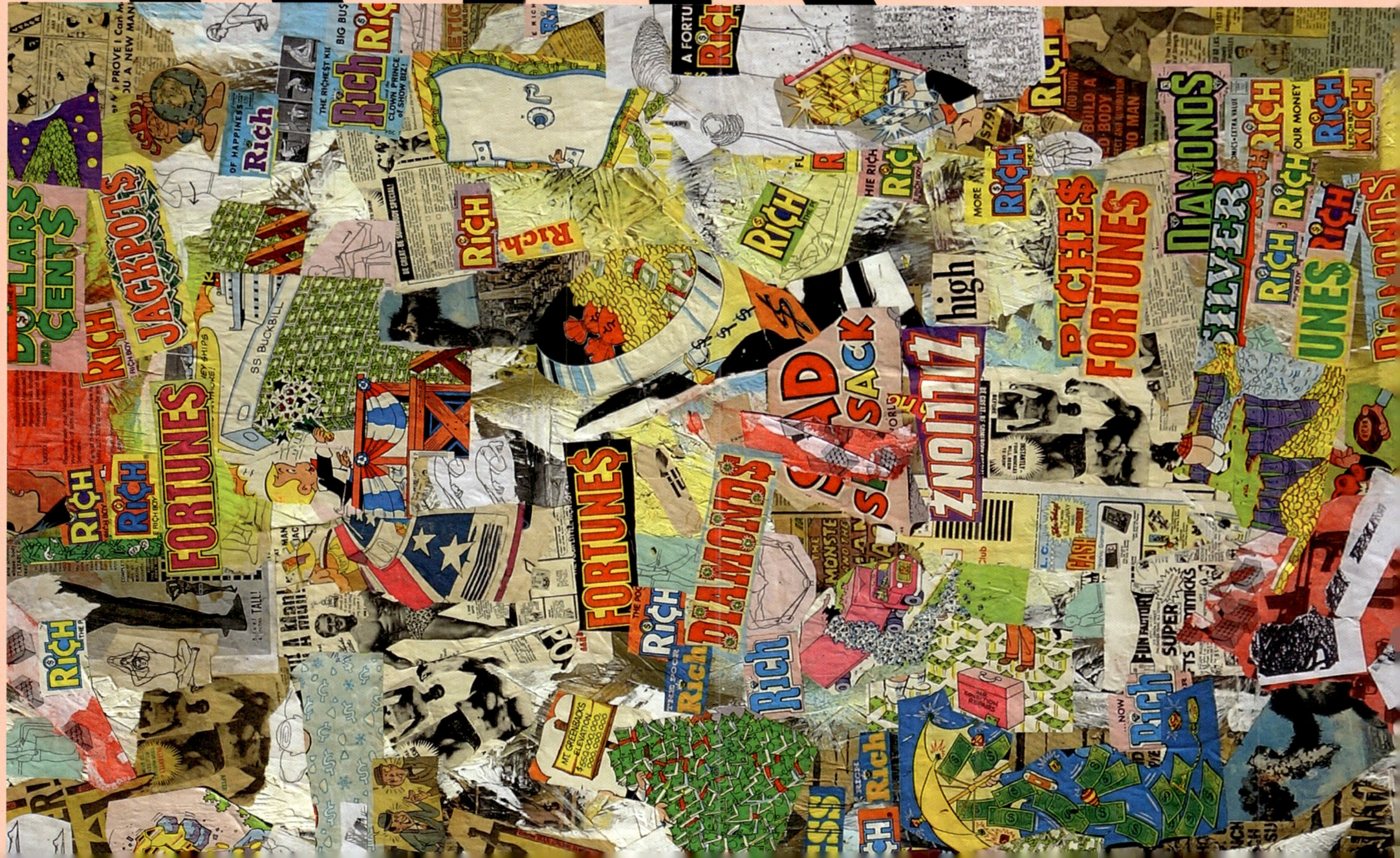

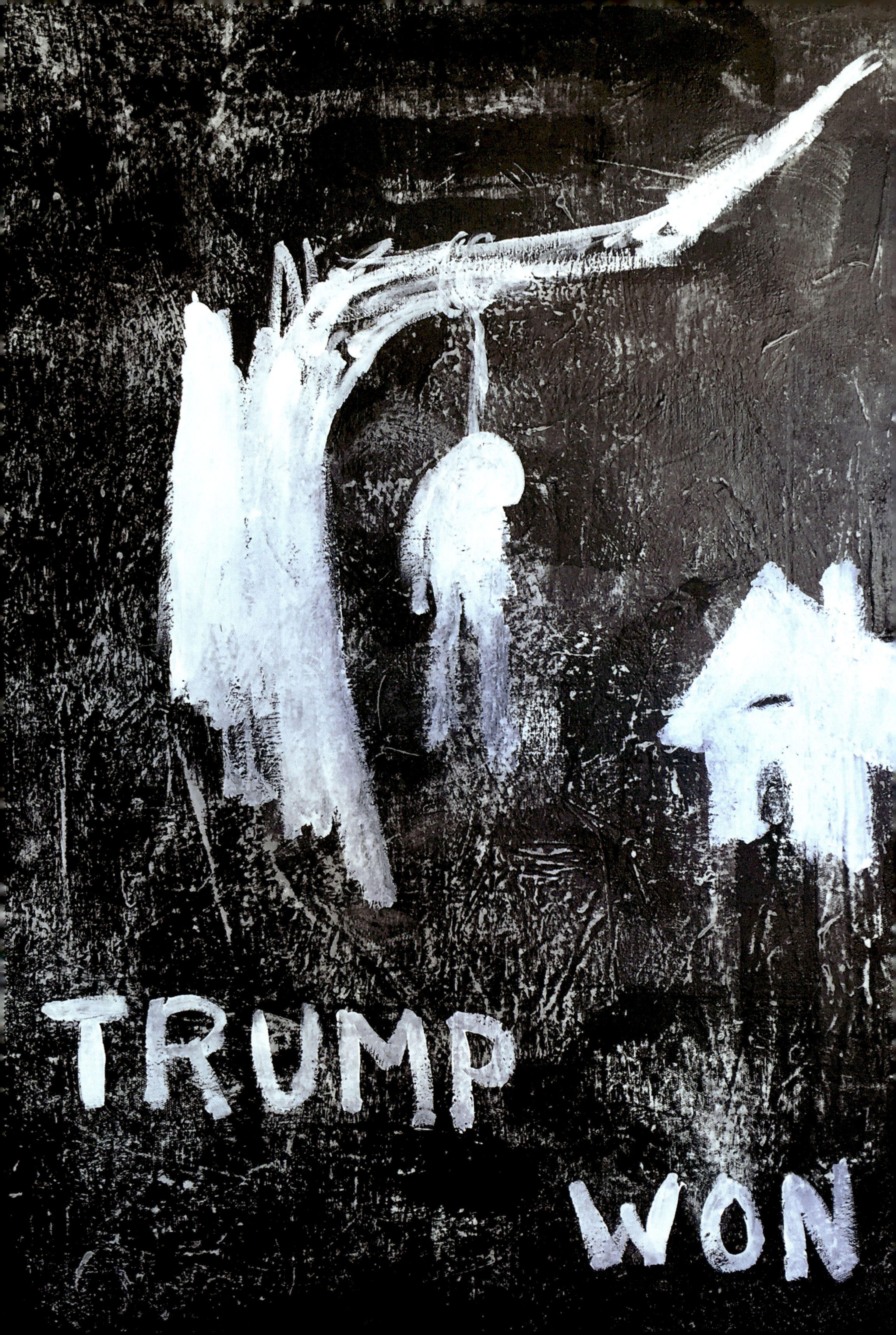
TRUMP
WON

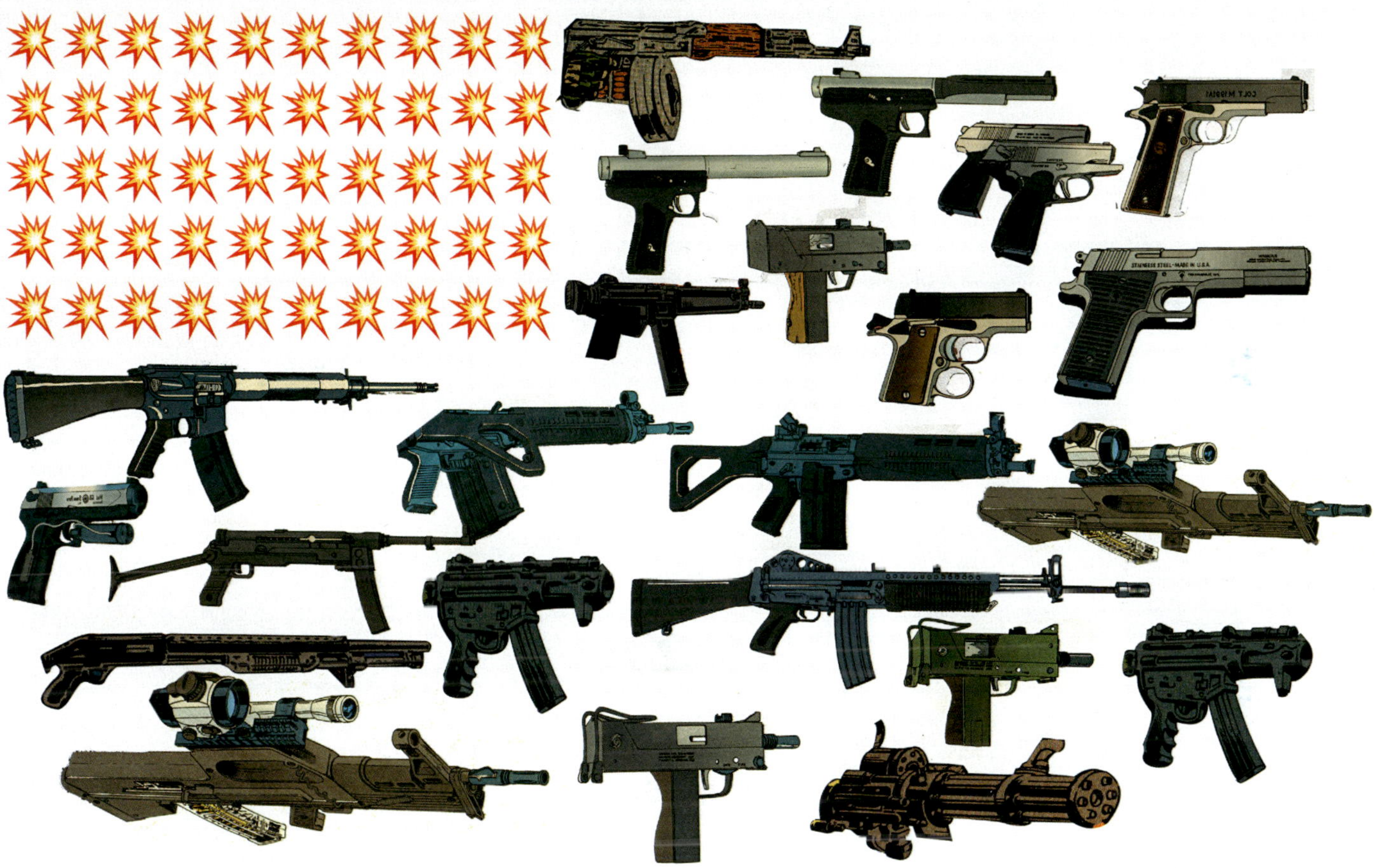

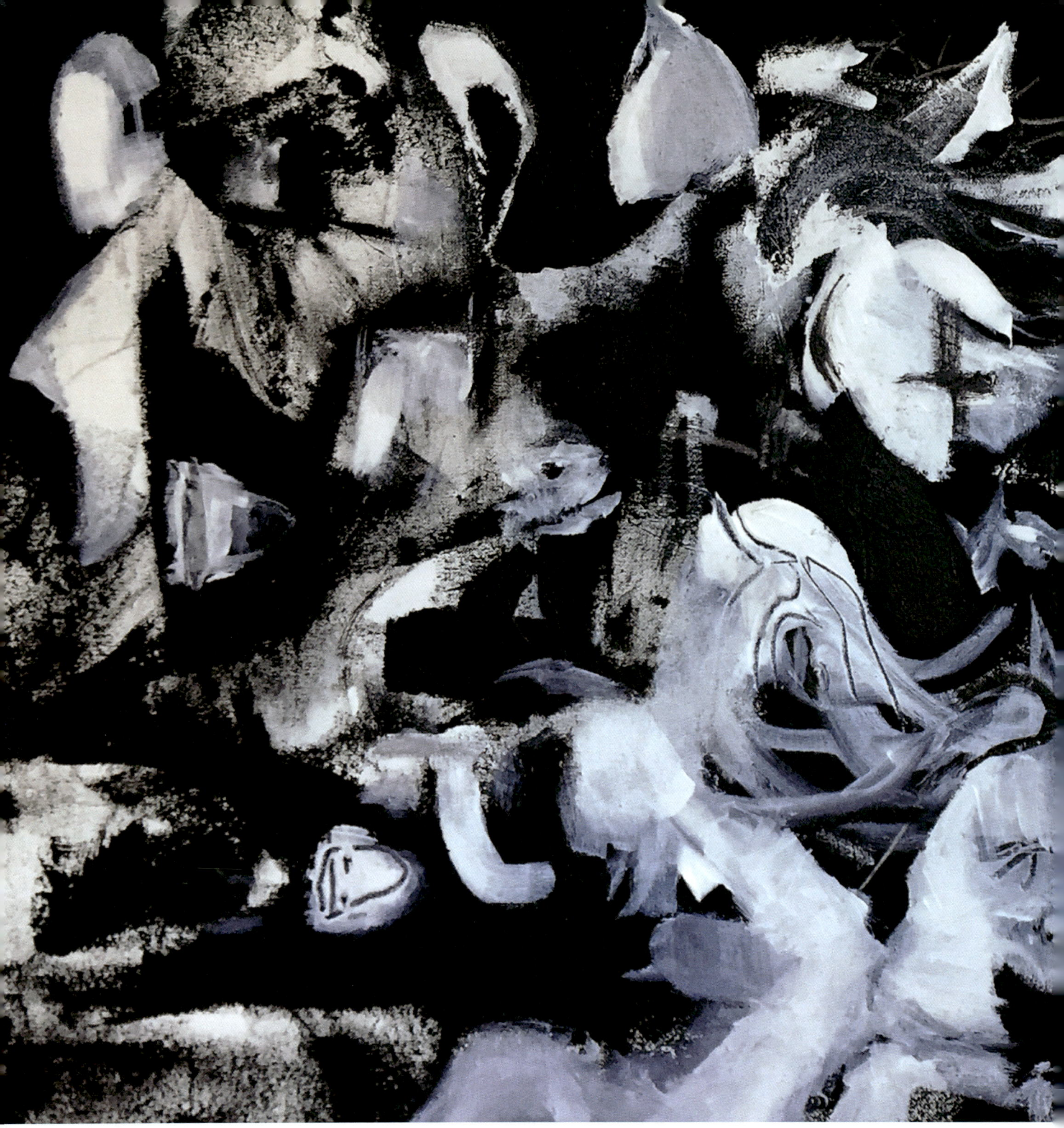

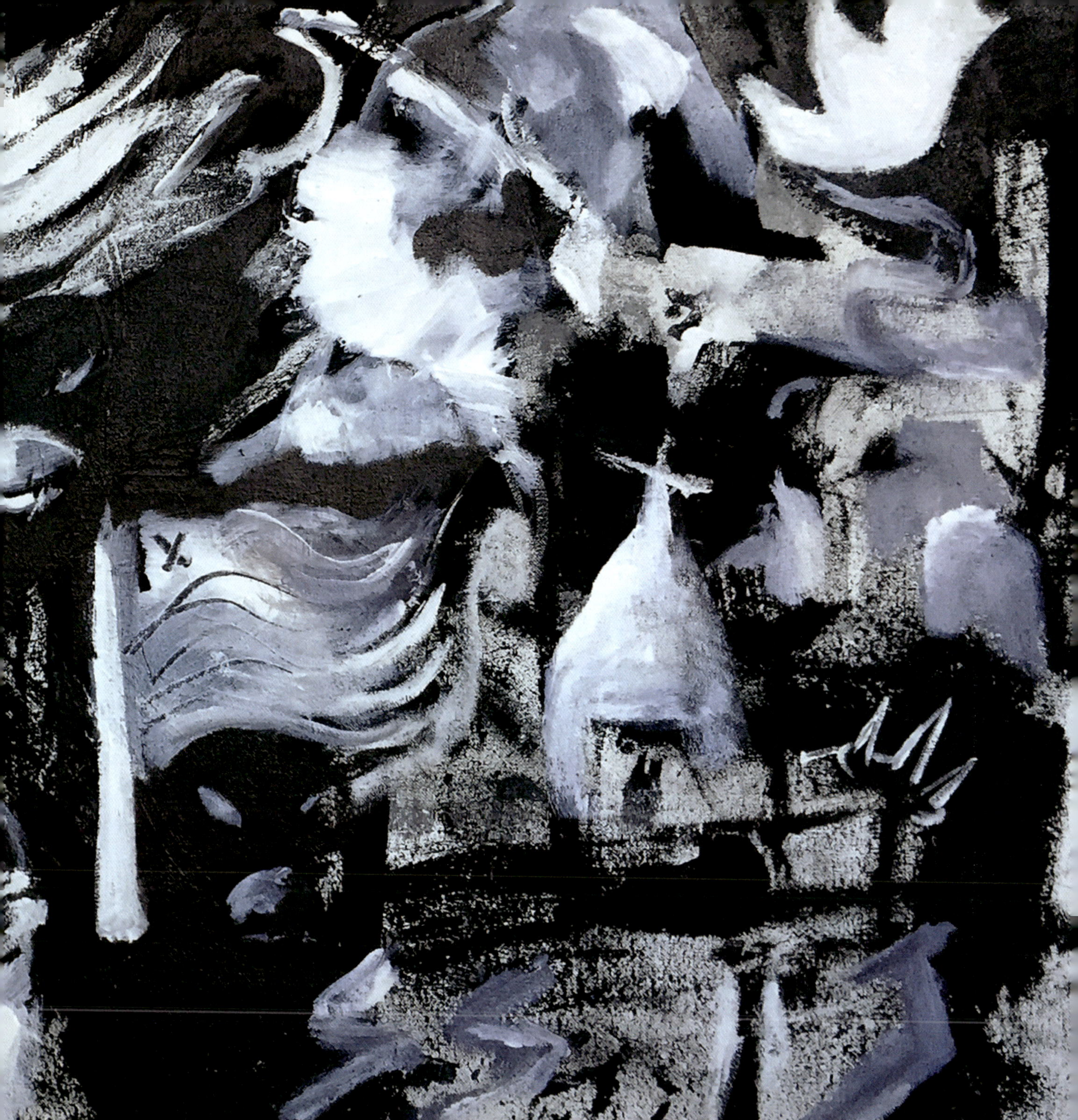

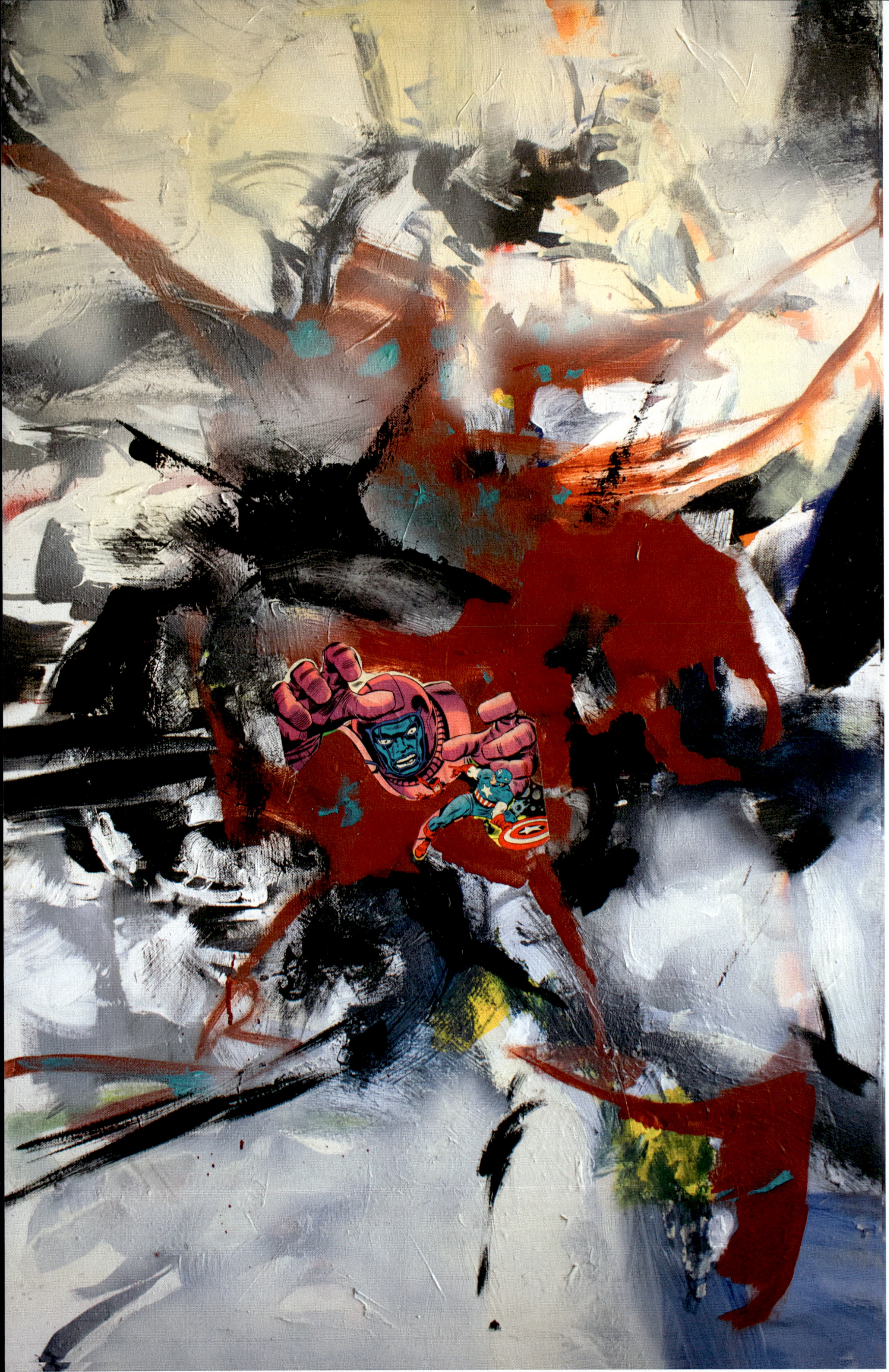

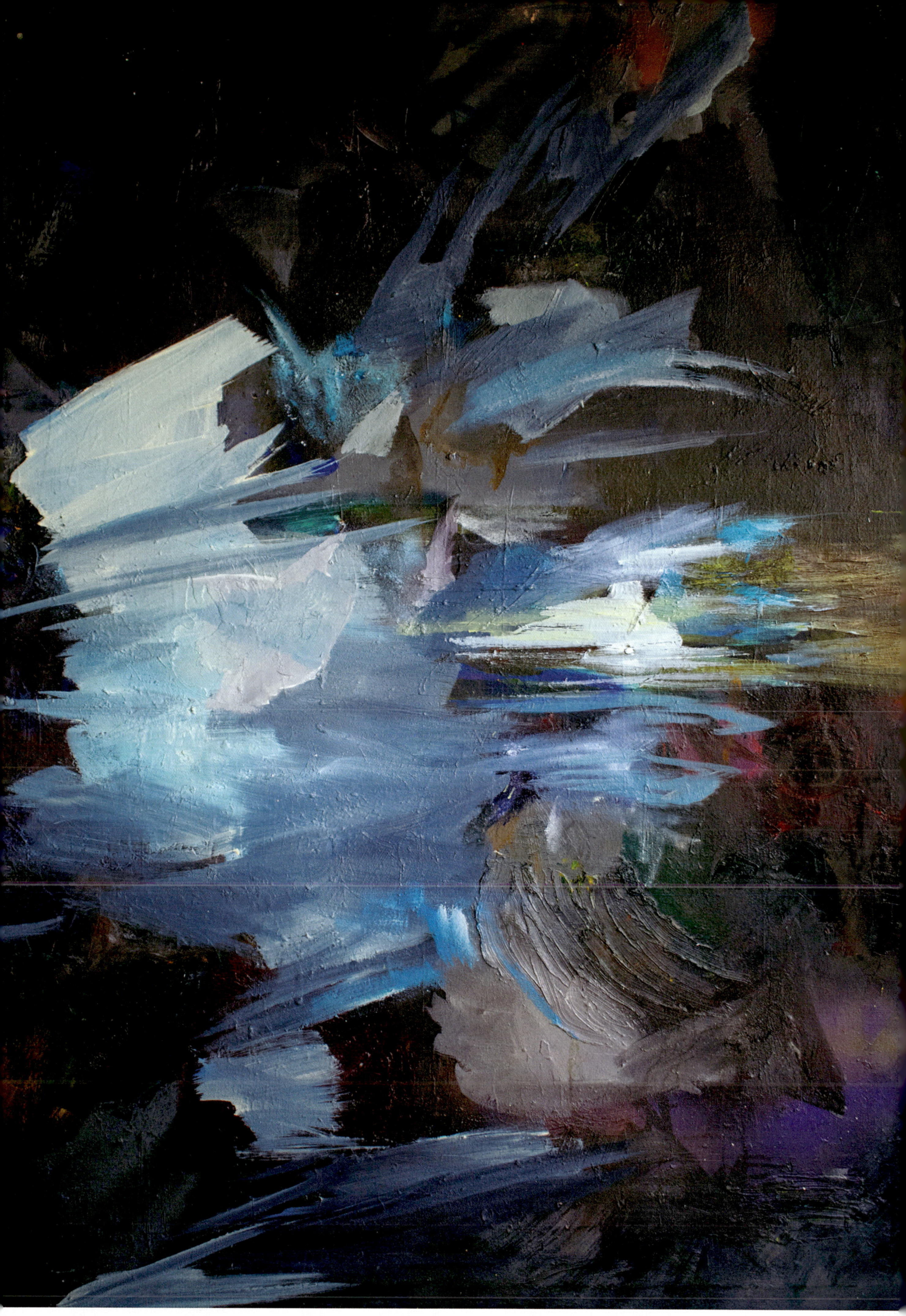

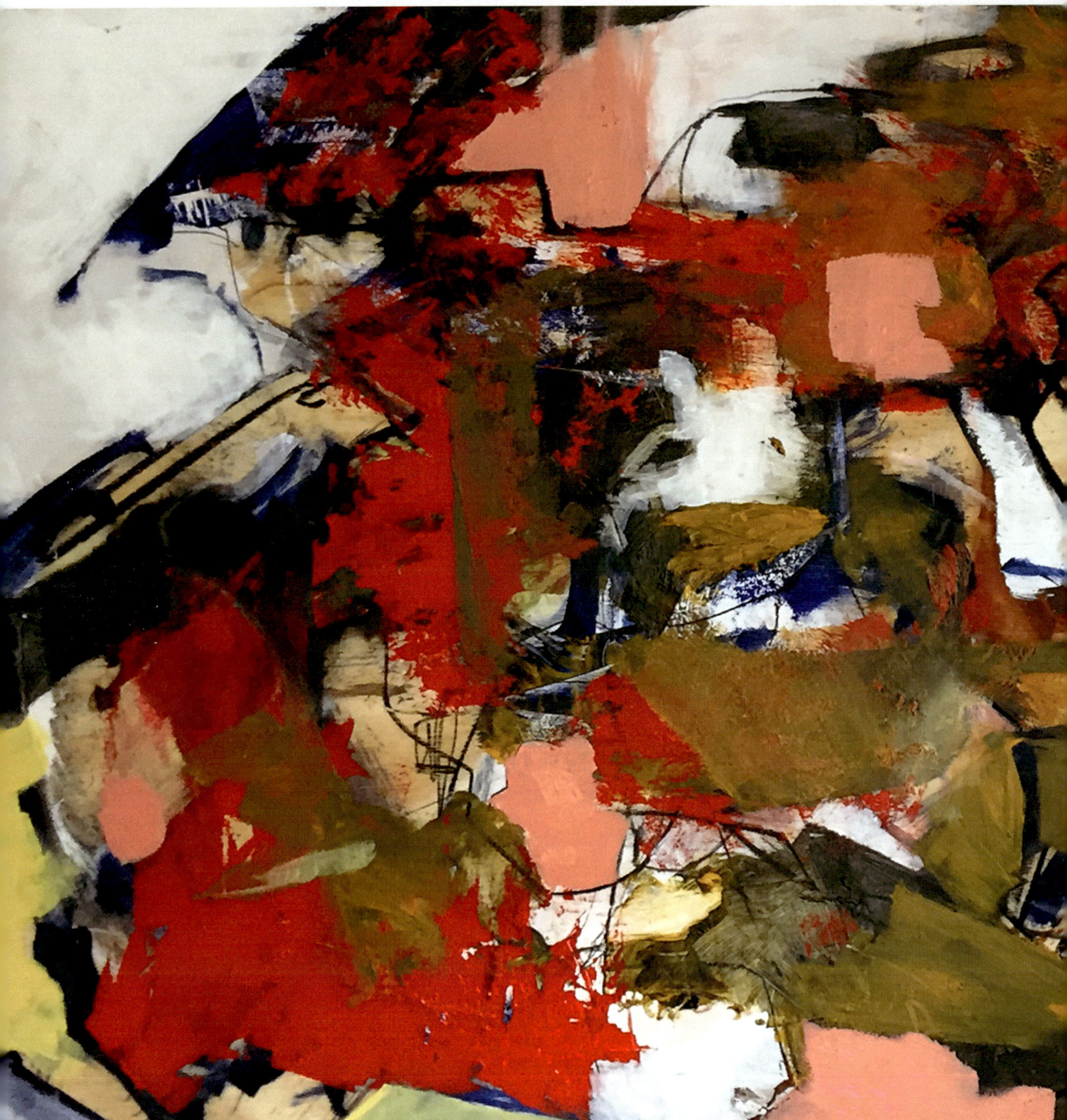

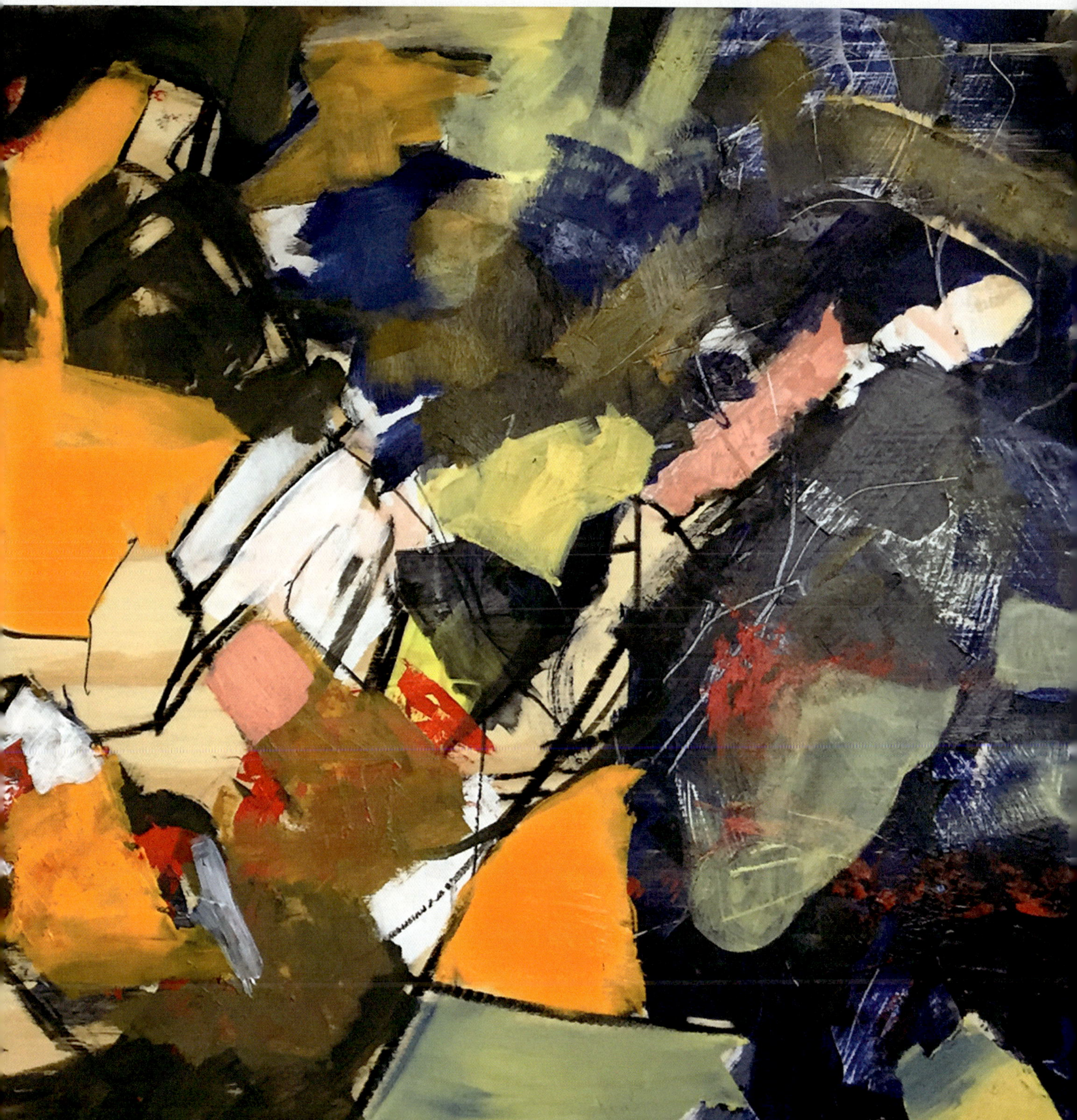

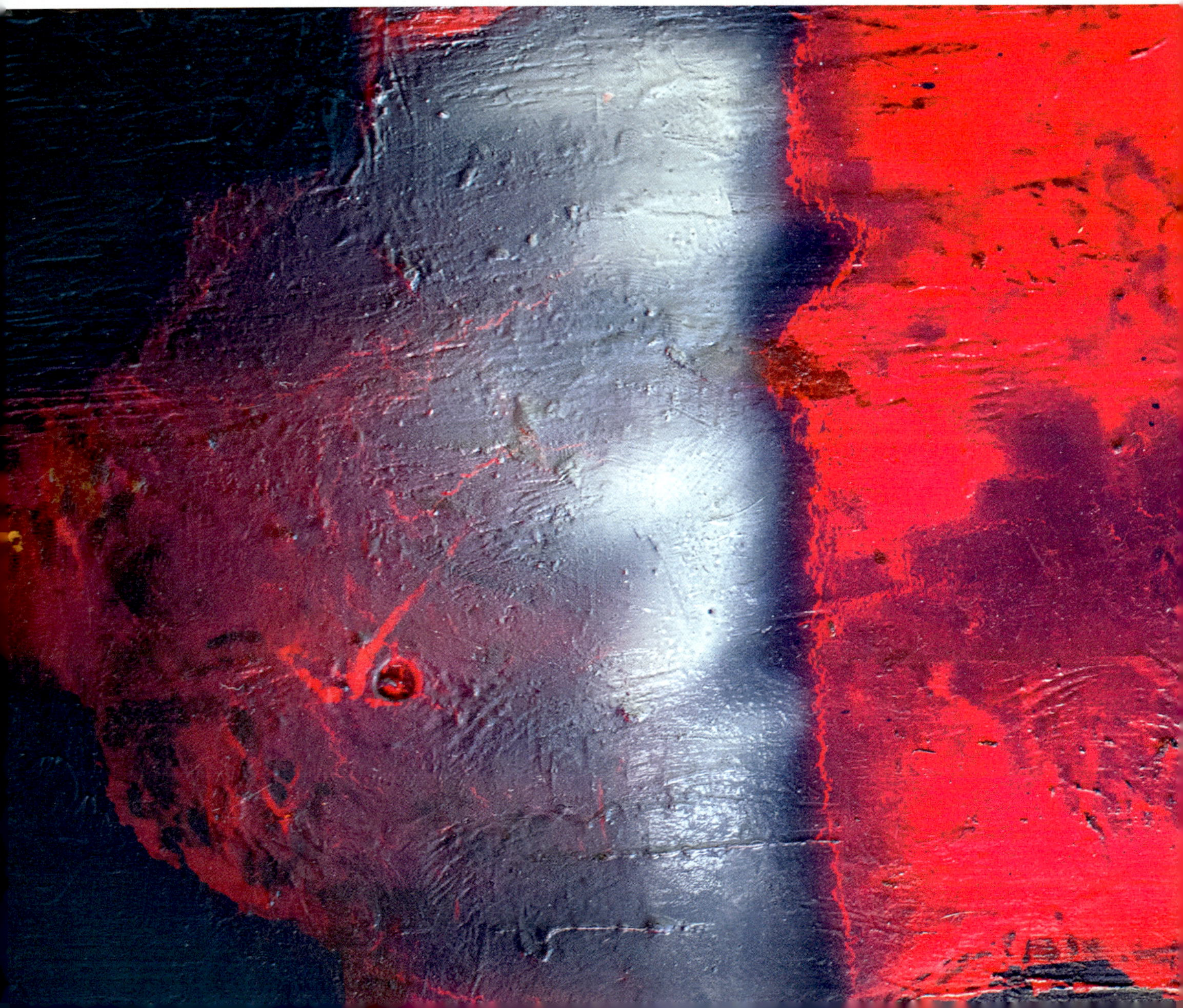

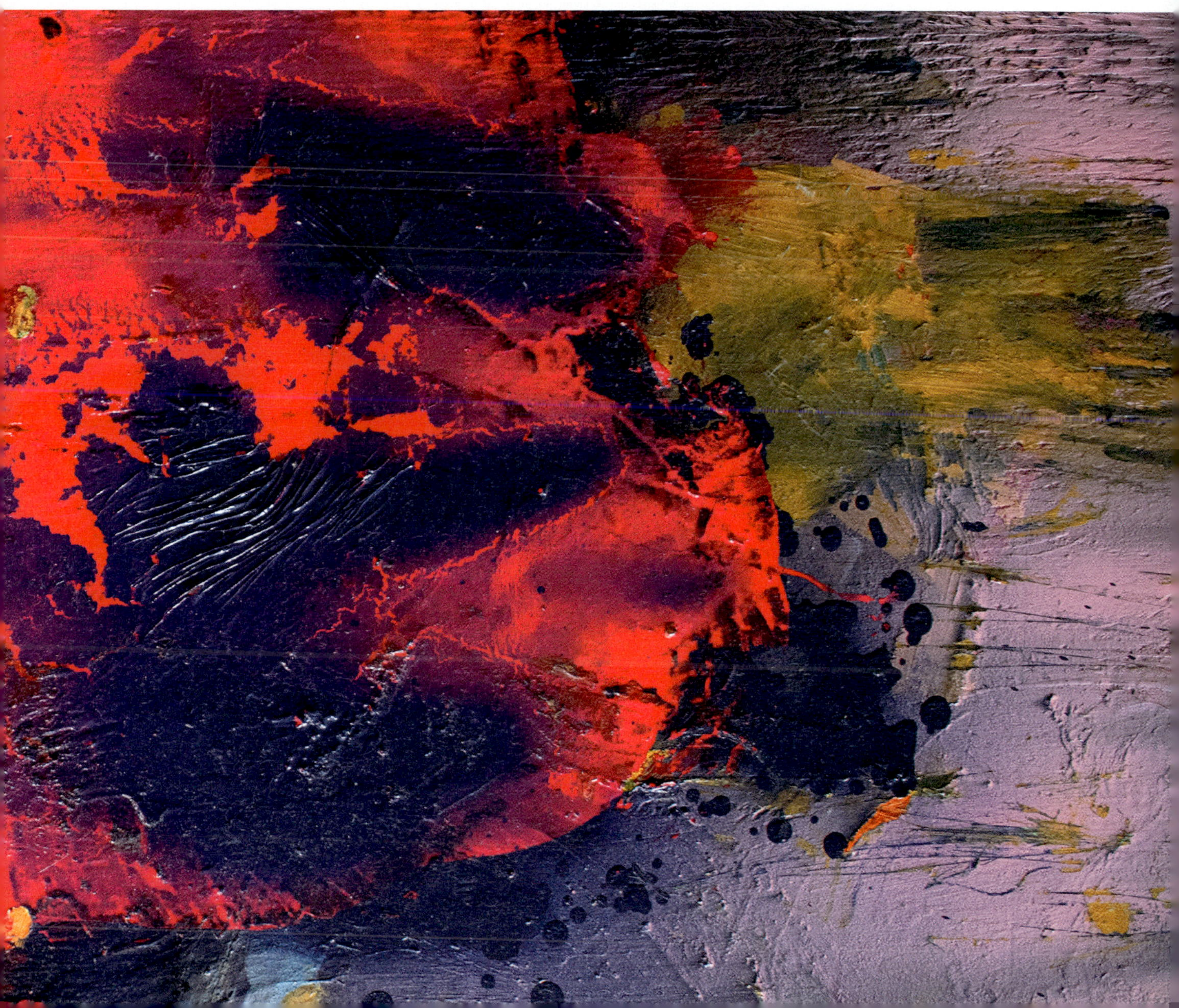

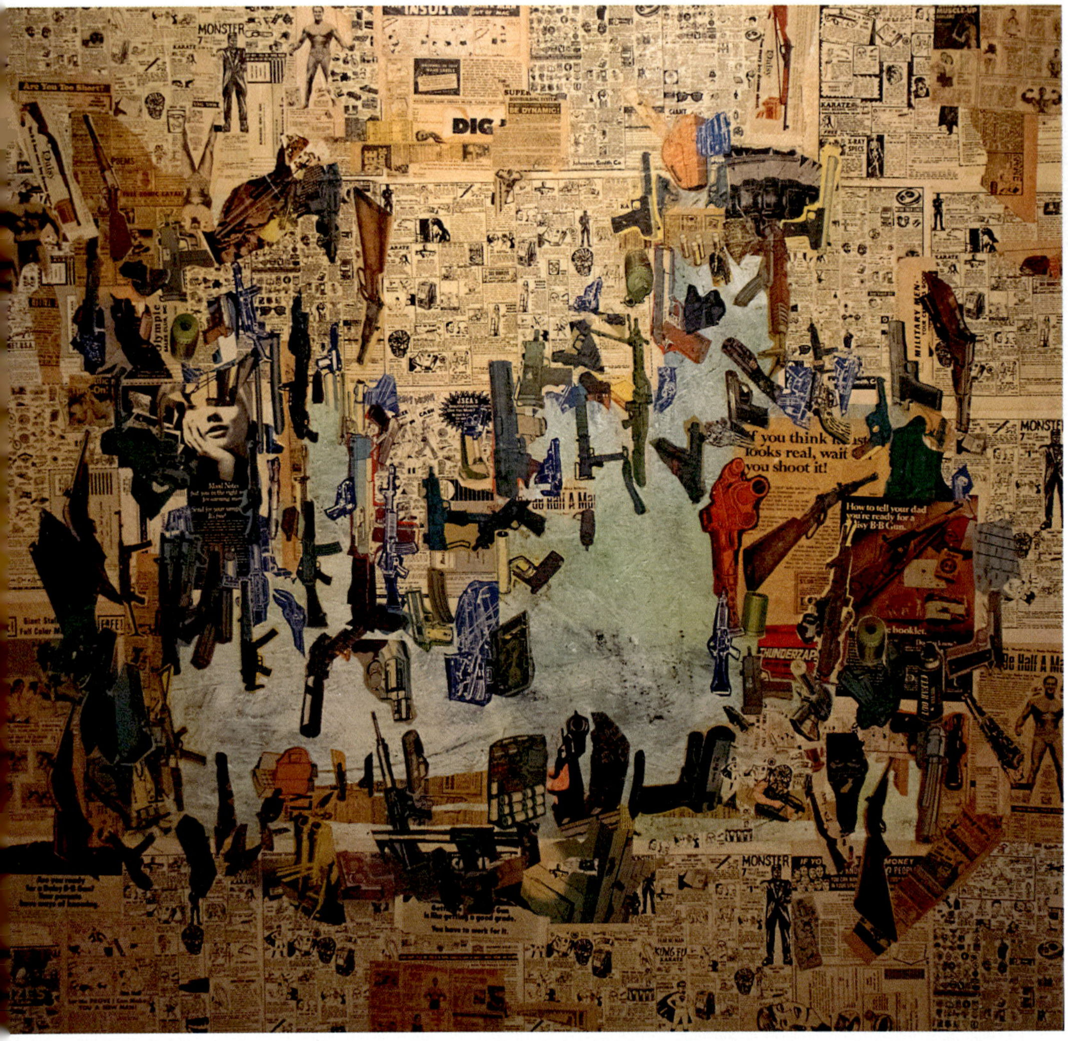

"Loquela–This word, borrowed from Ignatius of Loyola, designates the flux of language through which the subject tirelessly rehashes the effects of a wound or the consequences of an action: an emphatic form of the lover's discourse."

–**Roland Barthes**, A Lover's Discourse

VOMITORIUM OF ACQUIESCENCE

AN AFTERWORD

By pushing at the boundaries of American unease and examining certain discomforts, The Infected Nucleus (TIN) chronicles our divergent stages of experimentation and collaboration in our most vulnerable forms—while confronting our biggest crises. TIN is about "the self" pulling itself apart, battling and then ultimately accepting its solitudes, its struggles, the variable infections of its conditions. What results is not triumphant, but transformative.

As decency and discourse plummet in synchronicity with the condition of our planet, the rapacious nature of corporate culture exposes its most violent capacities. TIN is born from an impulse to acknowledge the normalization of the corrupt. Compounding assaults to our humanity manifest on many levels—mass shootings, for-profit prisons, institutionalized racism, neofacist propagandized media, a degrading environment, addiction, hijacked social systems, health crises, self-censorship, etc. All of which contribute to an unendurable cognitive dissonance.

TIN adopts the creative act as an analeptic response to living within these systems of normalized cruelties. It's offered as an artifact of defiance against the bubbles of self-delusion and denial, apathy and hatred. A curious offshoot from a polarized world of binaries. A cohesive salve formed between two artists fortifying themselves against the jarring madness.

// Robert and Daniel

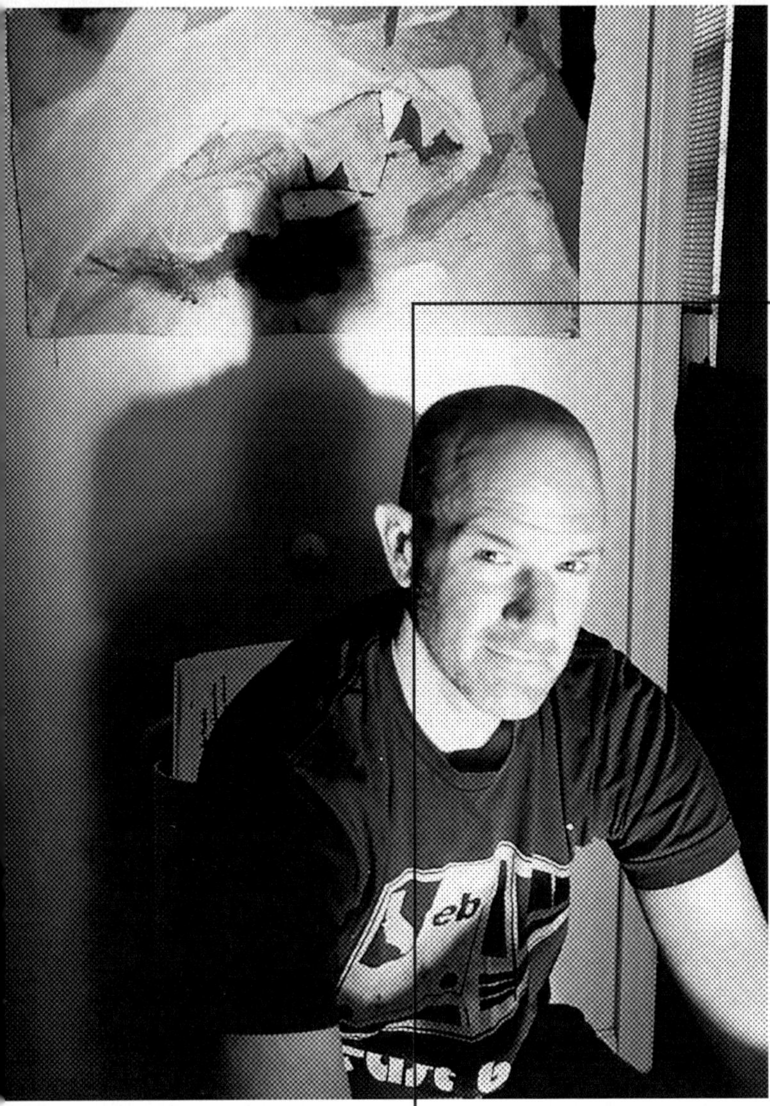

Daniel Cordani has received a BA in Psychology from the University of Delaware and an MA in Art Education from Brooklyn College. Through his multidisciplinary approach, he has exhibited work in galleries since 2000. In addition, he has remained active in the art community by facilitating art workshops, creating video projections for the Haiti Cultural Exchange, donating paintings to hospitals and designing art for independent music labels. Daniel began his mission of art as a tool for raising social awareness with the video "Evolutionary Threshold" which was premiered at the Newspace Gallery in 2005. He continues to develop work in an urgent voice that addresses environmental and humanitarian concerns.

Robert Booras received a BA from the University of Michigan, a MFA from Brooklyn College, and is currently completing a MSEd from Baruch College. He is the creator and editor of S.P.A.W.N (Sunset Park Art & Writing Newsletter), co-founder and managing director of UpSet Press, as well as a higher education professional and devoted advocate for students. He is the author of The New Night of Always (2016).

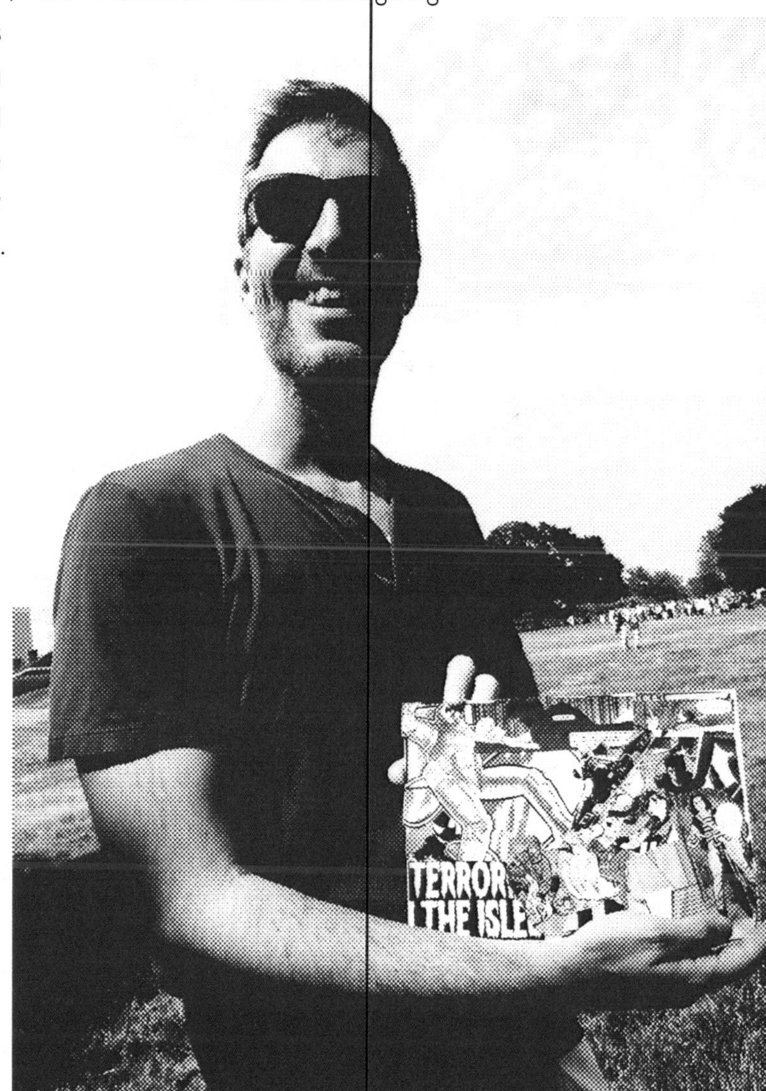

LOQUELA OF THE FATHER

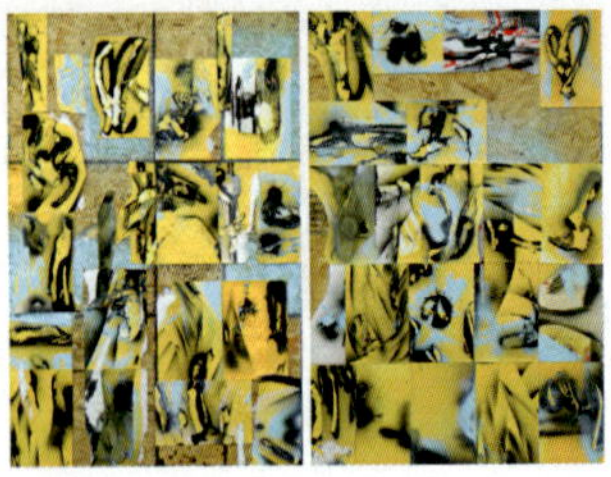

Prisoner of Conscience
36″x 48″(each panel, diptych) 2015
spray paint on comic book backing boards on wood chipboard

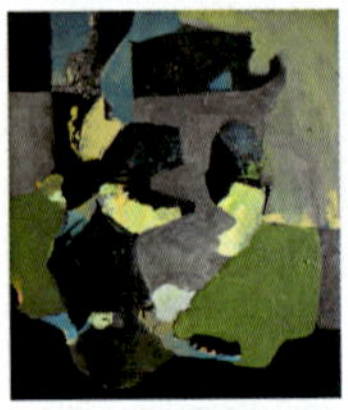

The Sludgie Parable
20″x 24″
oil & acrylic on canvas

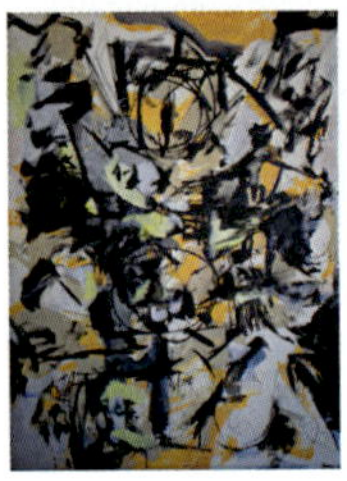

Silent Fury
22″x 36″ 2016
acrylic & graphite stick on paper

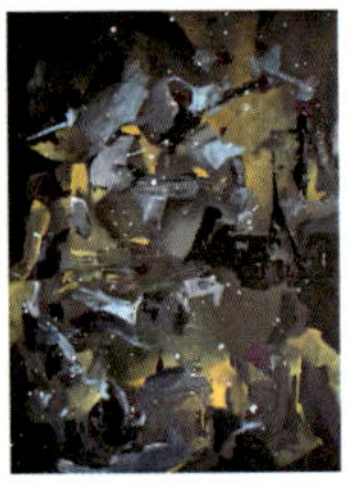

Silent Night, Surveilled Night
24″x 36″ 2017-2018
oil, acrylic & pastel on canvas

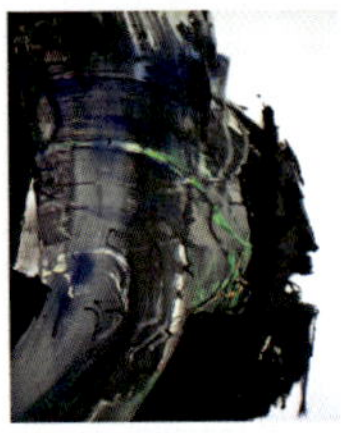

Jekyll's Hide
24″x 36″ 2010
oil, acrylic & spray paint on canvas

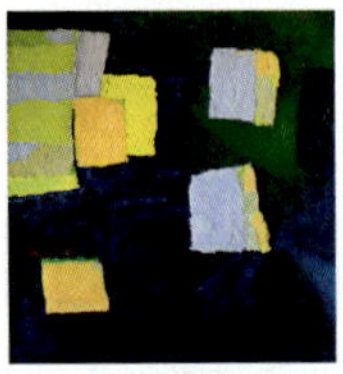

Pieces Don't Fit
30″x 33″ 2018
oil, acrylic & spray paint on canvas

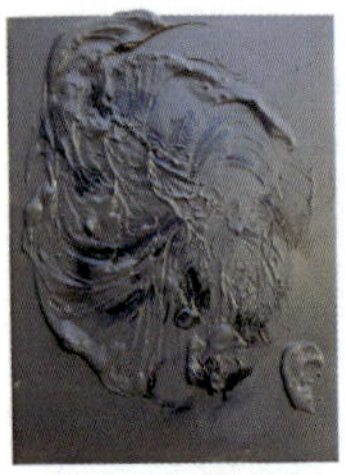

Popped Balloon
12″x 16″ 2017
acrylic, spray paint & water putty on canvas

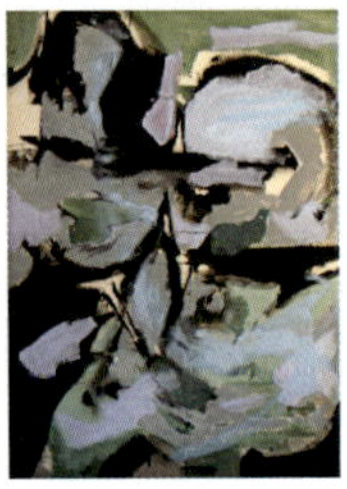

Skeptic
22″x 38″ 2014
acrylic & ink on canvas

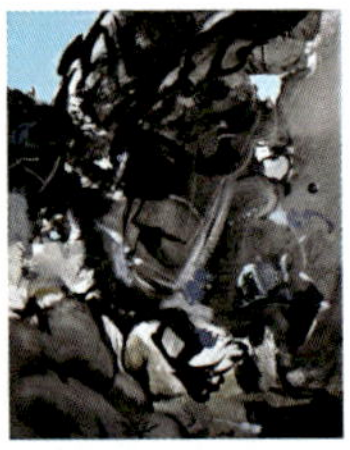

Revenge Billow
16″x 20″ 2017
acrylic & spray paint on canvas

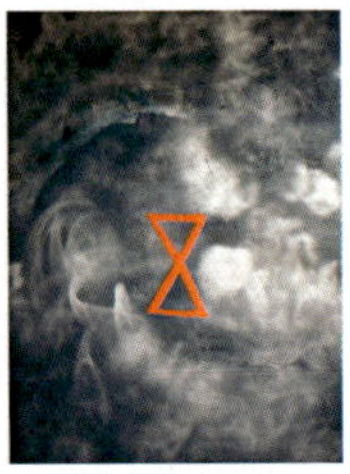

Extinction Rebellion
48″x 58″ 2019
oil, acrylic & spray paint on canvas

THE MOON

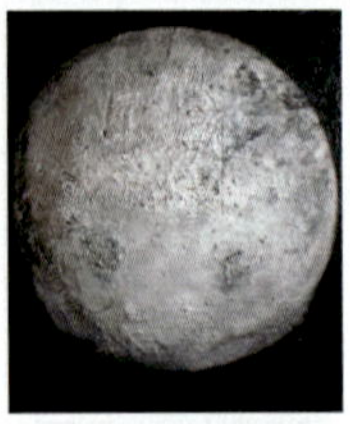

Fracked and Scorched
30″x 33″ 2018
oil, acrylic & spray paint on canvas

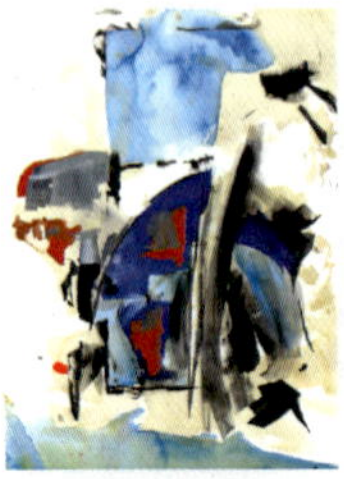

Escape Window
22″x 30″ 2014
ink & watercolor on paper

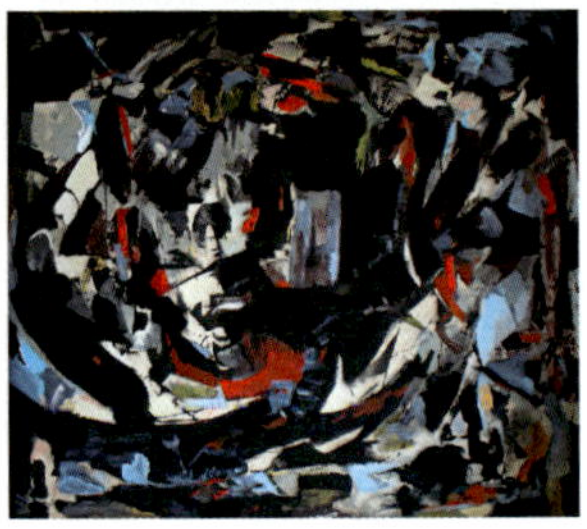

Infected Nucleus
45″x 48″ 2011-2019
oil & acrylic on canvas

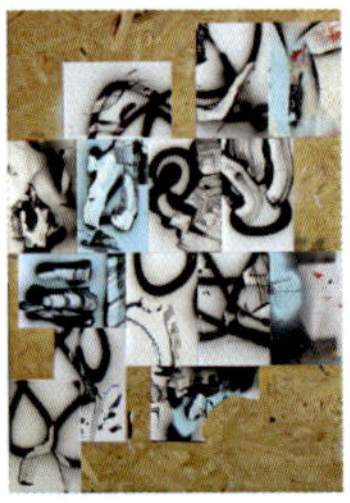

Profitable Neurosis
36″x 48″ 2015
spray paint on comic book backing boards on wood chipboard

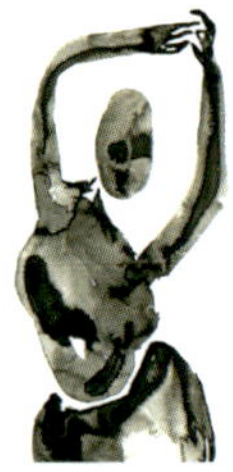

Dance
9″x 12″ 2016
ink on paper

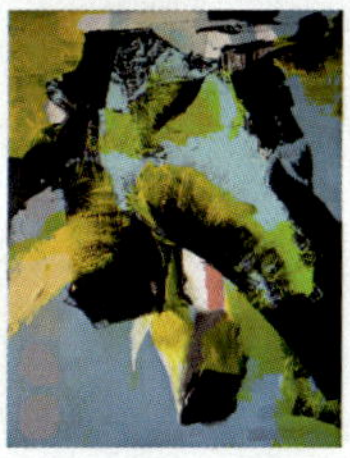

Brow
18″x 24″ 2017
oil, acrylic & spray paint
on canvas

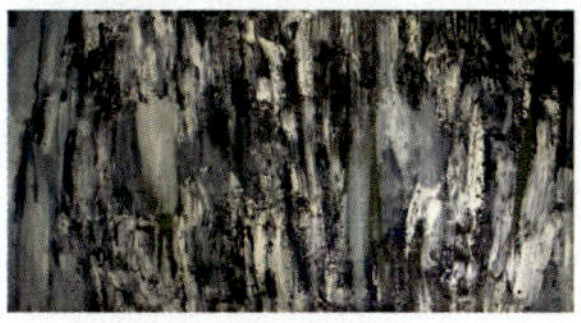

Silent Undertow
60″x 33″ 2017-2018
oil & acrylic on canvas

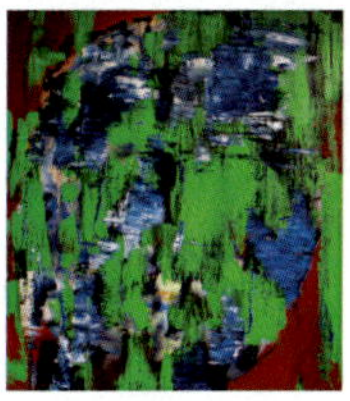

Planet Absent
35″x 41″ 2019
oil & acrylic on canvas

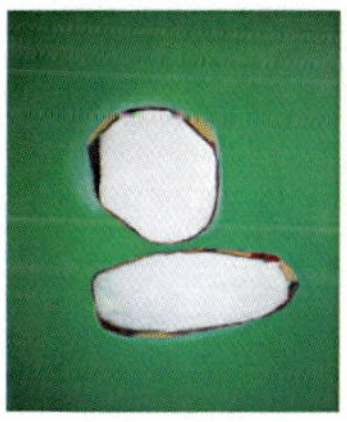

Signal Received
33″x 39″ 2018-2019
acrylic on canvas

GRAVIDITY

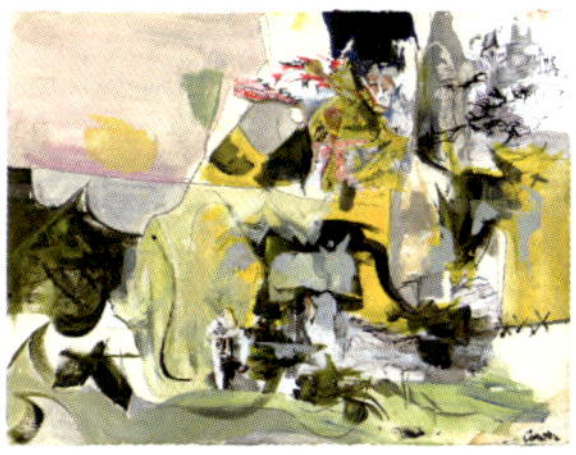

Untitled Fall
30″x 22″ 2019
watercolor, gouche, paper, ink
& marker on paper

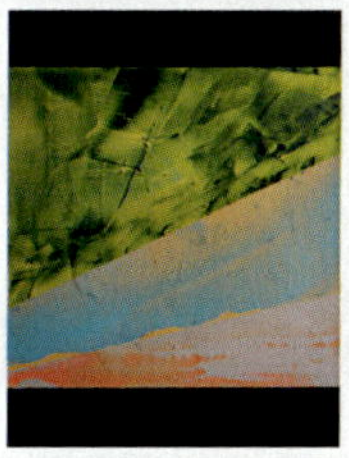

Beautiful Day (for nuclear war)
16″x 20″ 2016
acrylic & spray paint
on canvas

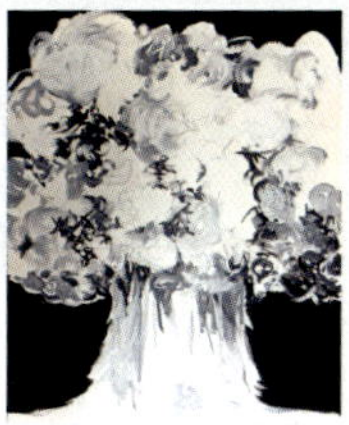

Bannon
18″x 24″ 2017
acrylic & pencil on canvas

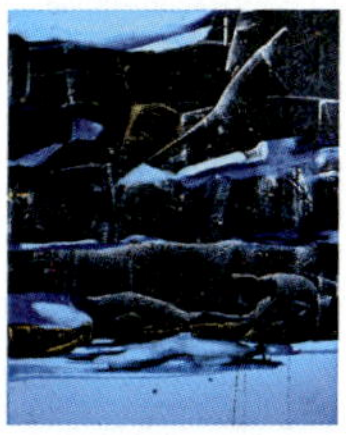

Blue Goodbye
16″x 20″ 2018
oil, acrylic & spray paint
on canvas

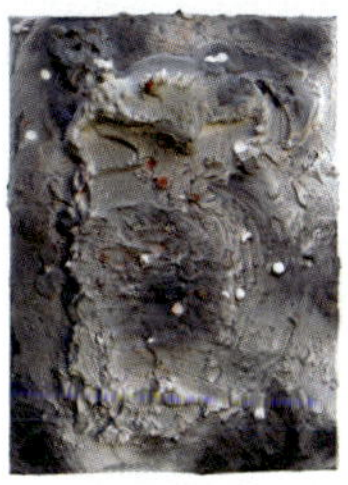

Waves it Comes
16″x 24″ 2017
waterputty, various pills
& spray paint on canvas

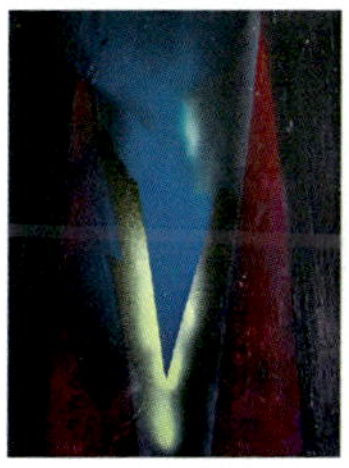

Fire on the Mountain
18″x 24″ 2017-2019
oil, acrylic & nail polish
on canvas

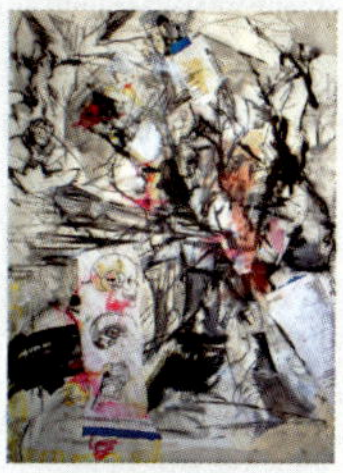

Head Scan
22″x 30″ 2016
graphite stick, acrylic, medical
test printouts & glue on paper

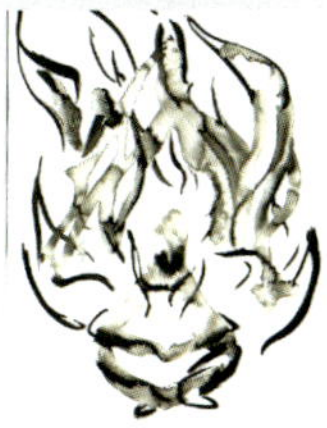

David Buckel
9″x 12″ 2016
ink on paper

Treated
24″x 60″ 2011-2019
oil, acrylic & spray paint
on canvas

THE CELL

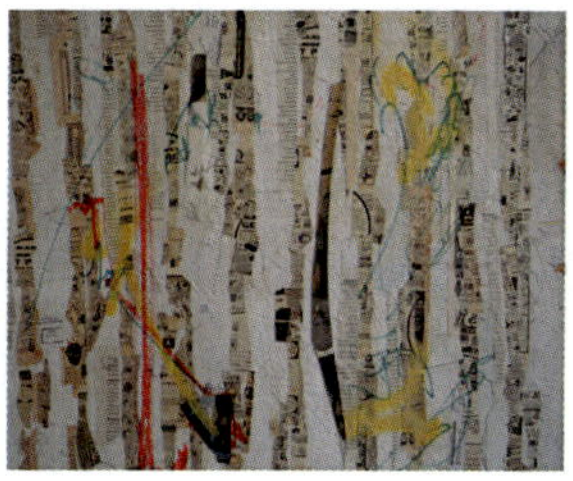

Consumer Cell
36″x 48″ (detail picture) 2017
acrylic, marker, vintage comic
book ads & marker on wood chipboard

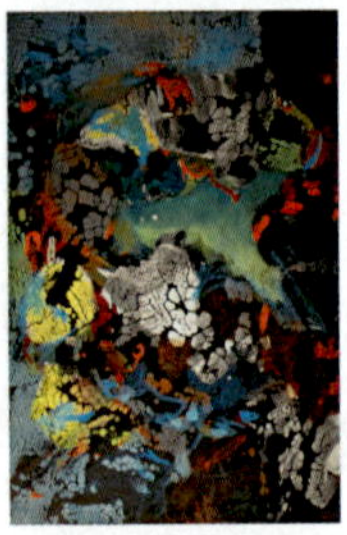

Shipwreck Diner
30″x 40″ 2017-2018
oil & acrylic on canvas

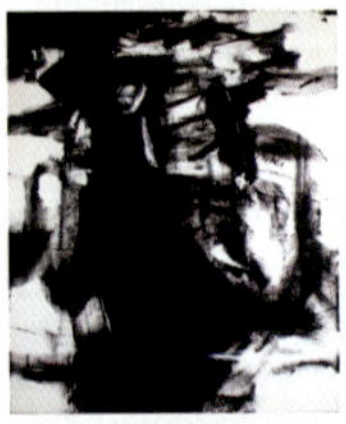

Disappointed Ancestors
18″x 24″ 2015
acrylic on canvas

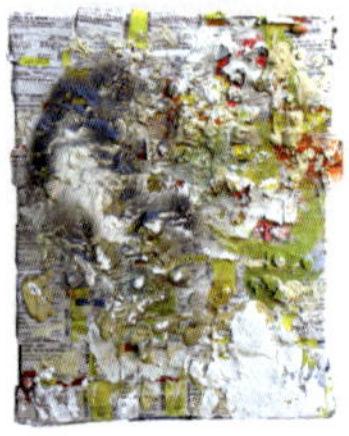

Fugue Topography
18″x 24″ 2014-2015
medication labels, various pills, water putty, acrylic & spray paint on canvas

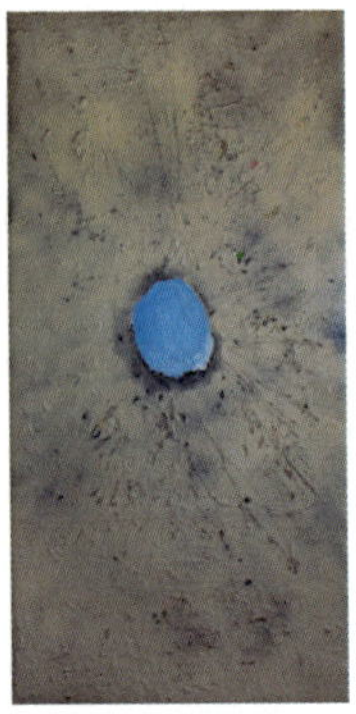

Fragile Clock
24″x 48″
oil, acrylic & spray paint on wood

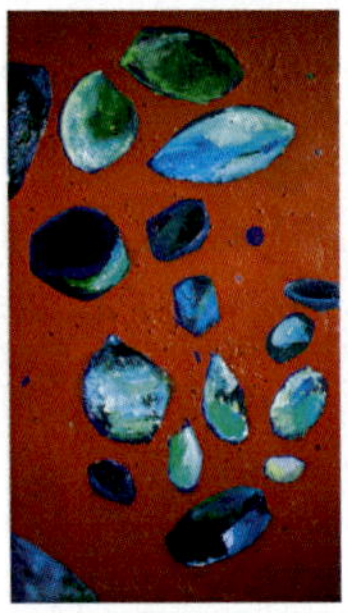

Rightful Owner Remembers
33″x 60″ 2017-2019
oil & acrylic on canvas

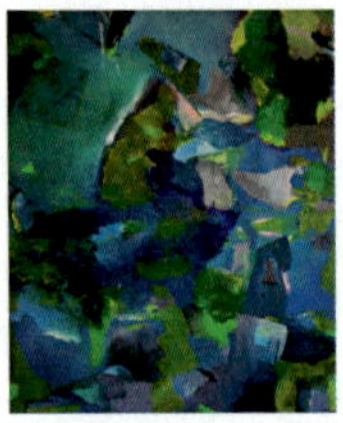

Bioplasticine Dream
41″x 52″ 2018-2019
oil, acrylic & spray paint on canvas

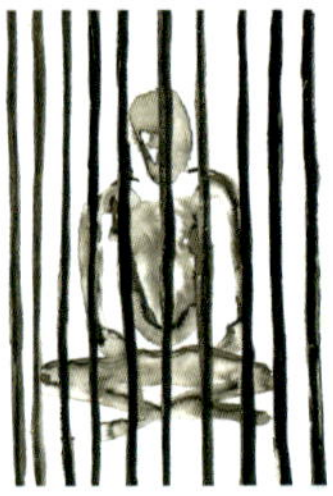

Innocent Meditation
9″ x 12″ 2016
ink on paper

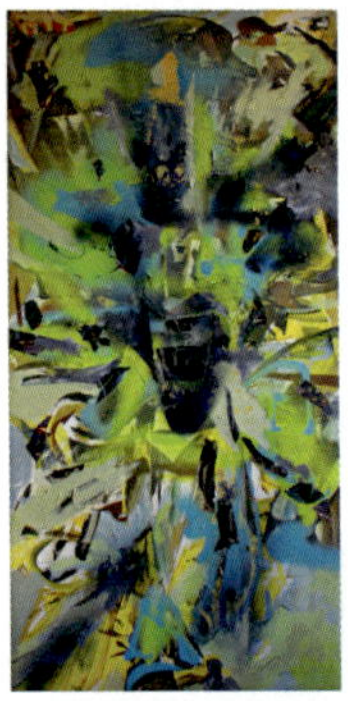

Shrapnel Flower
24″x 48″ 2016-2018
oil, arylic, marker & Punisher comics on canvas

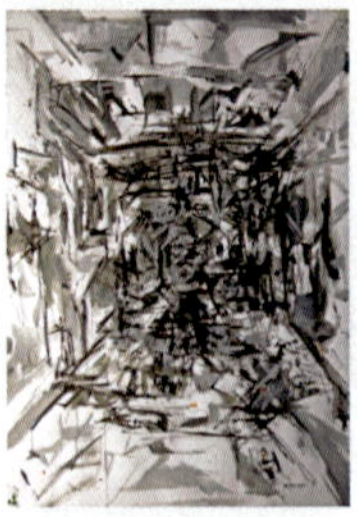

Beacon
22″x 30″
acrylic, ink & graphite stick on paper

TRUMP WON

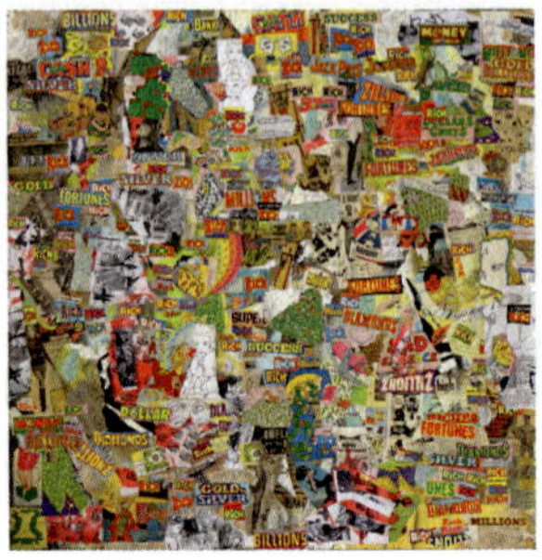

Moneyworld
48″ x48″ 2015-2016
comic books, printed paper, ink, marker on wood

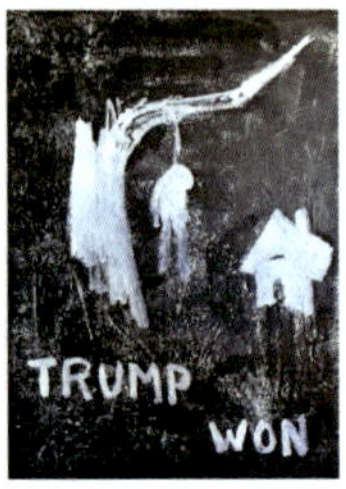

Won
30″x 40″ 2017-2018
oil & acrylic on canvas

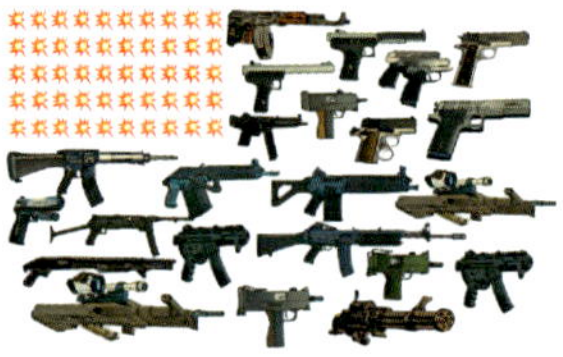

Erectile Dysfunction
10″x 8″ 2016
digital collage from Emojis & Punisher comics

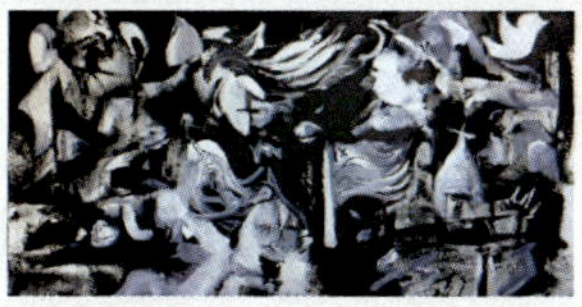

Twitler
48″x 24″ 2017
oil & acrylic on canvas

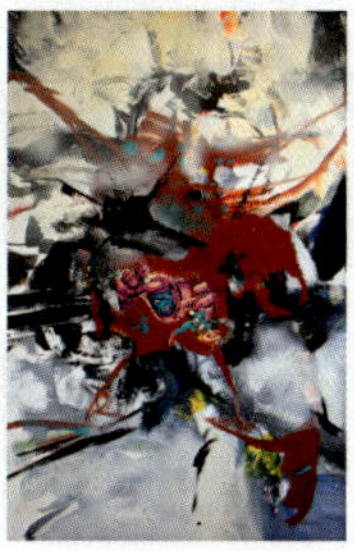

We Don't Want Your Help
24″x 48″
oil, acrylic & spray paint on wood

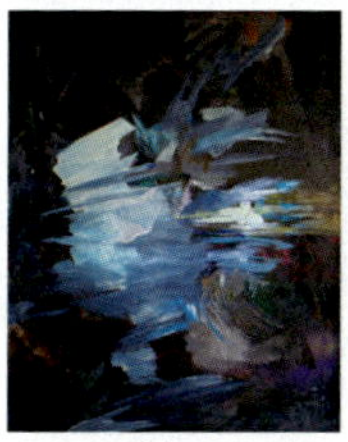

Inherent Glitch
46″x 60″ 2018-2019
oil, acrylic & spray paint
on canvas

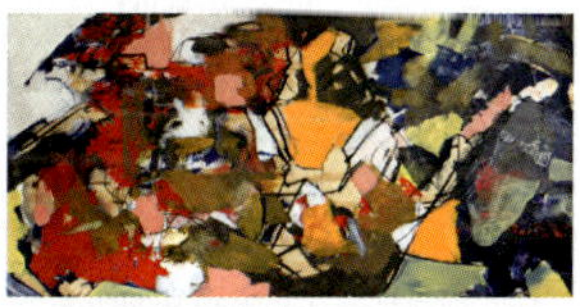

Fracked States
48″x 24″ 2015-2016
oil & acrylic on canvas

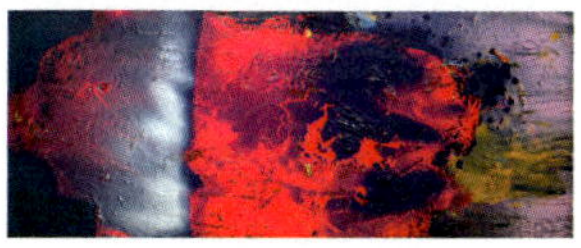

Sourced
38″x 20″ 2018-2019
oil, acrylic & spray paint
on canvas

Acknowledgements

Special thanks to Anselm Berrigan and the editors of Brooklyn Rail for publishing "Trump Won" in their December 2016/January 2017 issue, under the title "November 9th, 2016."

"Congratulations on your destruction" is a line (that is, refrain) from Hiromi Itō's poem, "Killing Kanoko."

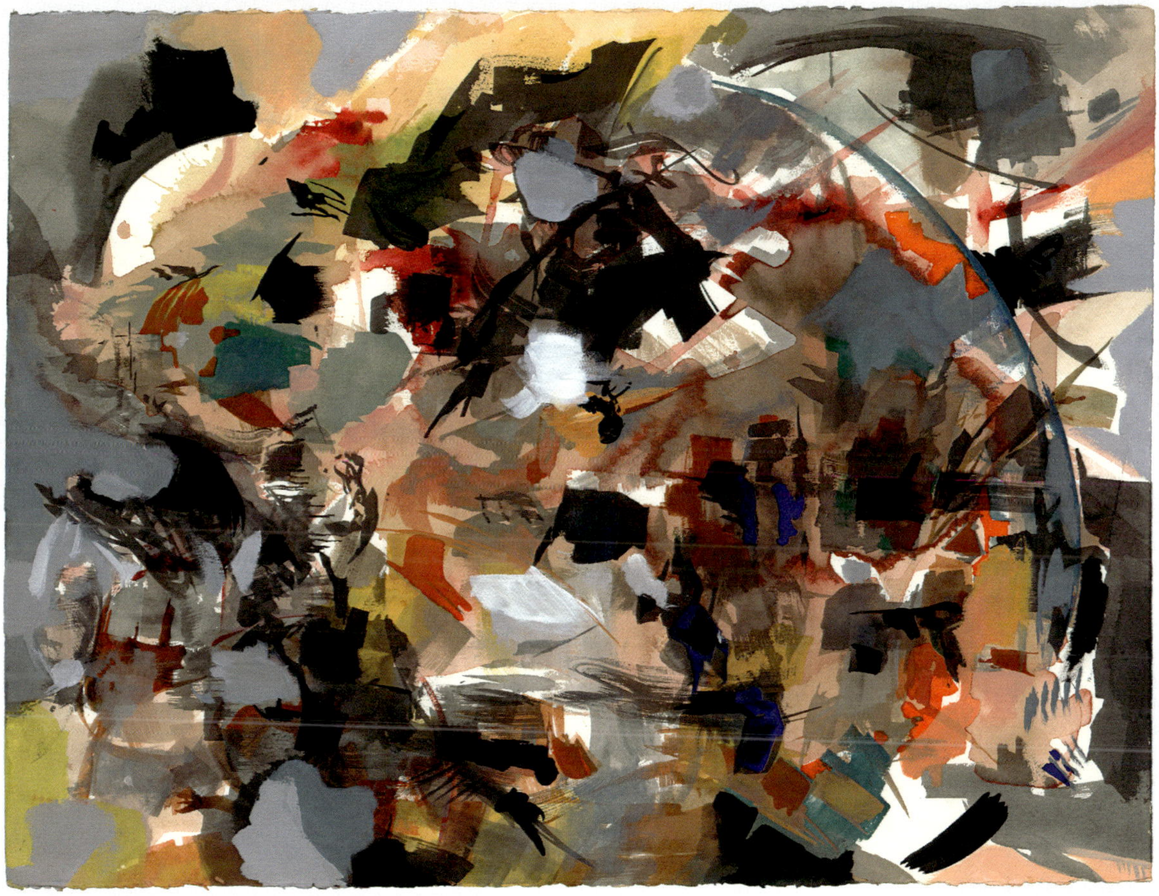

COVER PIECE

Spliced

30″ x 22″ 2014

watercolor & gouche on paper